AN INTRODUCTION TO PARANORMAL INVESTIGATION

by

KIERAN WOODHOUSE

Contents

Prologue

10… My head is resting on my chest and my arms are limp at my side.
9… I'm being told to focus on my breathing and relax my entire body.
8…
7… "Listen to my voice. Focus on my voice."
6…
5… My breathing is becoming deeper.
4…
3… My feet now feel like they are rooted to the ground.
2… "You should feel completely relaxed."
1…

The world doesn't seem to exist at this moment in time. My eyes are closed, my chin is resting on my chest and my body feels limp, yet strangely rooted to the ground that I am stood on. I am aware of myself and the voice that is talking to me. I am aware that there are people stood around me, some within close proximity. Some are there to simply view what is going on. Others are there for my safety.

The voice begins to talk, "Spirit, show me a yes answer…" A slight pause… "Thank you. Now show me a no answer…" Another pause… "Thank you."

Over the course of the next ten minutes or so, questions are fired at whatever spirit is interacting with us. Its instrument of reply is me. What we are doing here is known as the human pendulum and, in this instance, I am the pendulum. A voluntary pendulum, I must add. I soon wished I hadn't put myself forward. What feels like an open palm smacks me on the forehead and knocks me backwards with some force. Luckily, someone is behind me in case anything like this should happen. They caught me just before hitting the floor and helped me back to my feet. My head is killing me. It feels like it is trapped in a vice that is squeezing ever tighter by the minute. I can barely stand and I am taken from the room in to an empty one where I am told to focus on my helper's voice and nothing else. This becomes difficult when there are constant noises coming from behind me from an unknown source.

"What's your name?"

I stutter. Was it Kieran?

"What day is it?"

It's Wednesday. Definitely Wednesday.

"Wednesday."

"No, it's Friday."

This goes on for some minutes until my answers become clear and concise and we re-join the group. I'm told I was being thrown backwards and forwards in response to the questions. Apparently, according to some of the group I have spoken with since, I even managed the famous Michael Jackson lean with one response. I hasten to add here that I am over six foot and roughly nineteen stone. That kind of lean isn't an easy task if I was concentrating, let alone in the relaxed state that I was. Whilst I was in the adjoining room trying to calm down, the two of us heard a growl in the back corner of the room. Whilst it was a little disturbing, I tried to concentrate on relaxing after my human pendulum ordeal. What is interesting, though, is when we returned to the other room, the group in there had been asking questions and recording on an EVP recorder. When we all listened back to the recording, there was a clear "hello" being spoken. Furthermore, it seems that the timing of the "hello" coincided with the time that we had heard the growl in the adjoining room.

It seems I may have been interacting with some form of energy, spirit or whatever name you care to give it, and thus started my journey in to the world of paranormal investigations.

Beginnings

Ever since a young age, I have always had a fascination with anything that comes under the category of paranormal. Ghosts, aliens, Bigfoot and so on. Quite often as a child I would be too scared to sleep thanks to some book I had read or programme I had watched.

My parents had plenty of ghost stories to keep me entertained, too. Some were stories that they had heard from friends and family and some were first hand experiences. I intend to repeat some experiences that I have had and been told of throughout this book, and now seems like the right time to tell you of one of the earliest experiences that occurred in my family home.

The first home I lived in as a child was the top floor of a two-storey apartment building. The staircase that was used to access our home was our staircase alone, and it was located behind our front door, so was not used by the elderly couple below. My mum has always been house-proud and the house has always been adorned with ornaments here and there. The arrangement of the ornaments in our living room was exactly how my mum wanted them. Her late nan, however, often disagreed with the arrangement and would move them around in to different positions. It seemed that there was a constant tug of war going on between my mum and her nan, despite her nan having passed on several years before I was born. One night, we had been out. I can't remember where as I was very young at the time, but we had probably been out for a family meal or to a relative's house. Upon arriving home, my mum was shocked to find that the ornaments in the living room had been rearranged. Not only that, but they had been rearranged in the particular way that her nan would have arranged them back when she would visit regularly. This is just one of the many events that occurred in this home. Quite often, the child gate at the top of the stairs would bang loudly. I remember lying on the living room floor one evening, with some crayons and a book, when the gate began to bang. Initially frightened of the loud noise, I had asked my mum what the noise was. Her response was that it was just her nan letting her know that she had left the child gate open, which isn't ideal for a stair gate that is used to prevent children from falling down the stairs.

Back when her nan had died, before I had been born, my mum had purchased some black leather gloves as a present for her nan. When she passed away, my mum thought it would be a nice idea to wear them to the funeral. When she had gone to fetch the gloves from her bedside cabinet, she couldn't find them. Along with my dad, they searched high and low for the gloves, my mum being quite upset at the prospect of having lost them on that day in particular. Eventually, they had to concede that they were not going to be found and my mum attended the funeral of her nan without the gloves. The day after the funeral, whilst looking for the gloves again, she found them exactly where they should have been all along, in the bedside cabinet.

She assures me that both herself and my dad searched everywhere for the gloves and that they were most certainly not in the bedside cabinet.

As I grew older, my fascination grew also. I was always looking for the next piece of evidence or theory to "blow my mind". My interests began to take different forms, too. No longer was I just interested in ghosts. Now I wanted to understand UFOs, conspiracy theories and so forth. Unfortunately, as happens with most people, life tends to get in the way. Get a job, find a house and not have enough time to follow your passion, or in my case, continue my research. One event got me back in to this field though and it wasn't a particularly nice event, to say the least.

One sunny afternoon in 2011 in Coventry, whilst playing rugby, an awkward tackle forced me one way, leaving my leg the other. The pain was excruciating. After many hospital visits, I found out that I had torn the medial ligament and posterior ligament in my knee, popping a cartilage, also, for good measure. This ended in a six-hour operation and ten weeks in a wheelchair. As you can imagine, this meant that I now had a lot of spare time on my hands and a lot of sitting on the sofa watching TV (gaining weight drastically!). At this time, I discovered a programme called Ancient Aliens. A couple of episodes of this and my passion had been reignited. My thirst for knowledge was as great as it had ever been.

With my renewed passion I began to attend paranormal investigations. These were as a paying customer with several different organisations that ran paranormal events. Some were good and I enjoyed them, but some were a bit of a disappointment. I felt, at times, that we were being led to see, hear and experience things that weren't actually there to see or hear. Some groups even have a group medium who is there to help guide the guest through the evening. Whilst I do have a belief that mediums do indeed carry a talent of sorts for conveying messages from "the other side", I couldn't help but feel that some of these were in place to create the power of suggestion within the minds of the paying customer. After all, these groups rely on paying customers to keep them going, so they need to ensure that the customers have an entertaining enough night to want to return and pay for another evening of entertainment. I didn't like this approach at all. However, as I say, some were good. These were the groups that would let you experience the night for yourself. They would allow you to immerse yourself in the atmosphere of the building that you were investigating and make your own conclusions from whatever evidence you had collected, if any. I add the "if any" because there are some investigations that leave you feeling disappointed or empty. Yes, this can be very frustrating, but anyone looking to head in to this field needs to understand that it isn't constant activity every time you step in to an investigation. In fact, I'd say that roughly 95% of time spent on a paranormal investigation is full of inactivity, with the remaining 5% of time being immersed in activity, such as noises, feelings, senses and so on. However, out of that 5%, a further 4% can be explained away by simple explanations, such as a draughts or tired guests making noises. Unfortunately, certain TV shows have led people to believe that those percentages are the other way around, with it being active 95% of the time. What people need to remember, though, is that a TV show is around 45 minutes long, and the producers and hosts need to keep the viewer entertained. It would be no good airing a show where the participants are sat in a dark room, in silence, with nothing happening. Not only would this not be entertaining in the slightest, but the viewer wouldn't think twice about not tuning in again the following week. Now, I am not for one second trying to say that these shows are faked (although there is enough evidence around, particularly on the internet, to show otherwise), but as soon as a paranormal team have a television series, their number one priority no longer lies with trying to find evidence of paranormal activity. It lies with their ratings and what it is that will keep the viewers watching week after week, and ultimately keeping them in a well-paid job.

Eventually, I was lucky enough to be asked to join a paranormal team myself. This was a huge opportunity for me and one that I couldn't turn down. It has allowed me to conduct investigations, along with the rest of the crew, to a standard that we believe is right. Some events we have the public with us. For these events we let them lead us, so to speak, as they are the paying customer. Lessons learned from previous teams meant that it was important to us that we didn't, in any way, push the guests in to seeing or hearing things. We simply set up experiments and allowed the guests to have their own experiences. Other events we have crew only, where we allow our investigations to travel a little deeper, throwing up some very interesting results which I will discuss throughout this book. The reason I say we go deeper as crew only is because although we understand that misleading guests is in every way wrong, we also understand that guests have paid and do expect an eventful night. In no way does this mean that we fake experiences for the benefit of the paying customer, but it means we maybe won't spend as long in one location as we might if it were just crew alone, as the customers may want to move on to the next location.

Over recent years, besides the paranormal investigating, my biggest fascination has been with the nature of reality and how, and why, we perceive the world as we do. Understandably, a lot of people wouldn't think of linking this research with that of the paranormal. However, in my opinion, it is not only linked, but one and the same. Some people, myself included, describe a spirit as something that can interact with us and affect things within our "perceived" world, such as communicating on a spirit board or by touching someone or by moving an object. A ghost is described as a recording, where the ghost will carry out the very actions from when they were alive. For example, the reason they can walk through walls may be because that wall was never there when they were alive. Another example is when they are seen floating above the ground. This could be because the ground was higher back when they were alive. All of this whilst paying no attention to the living world around them. This certainly makes sense to me.

My recent research has led me to ask the question: Given that everything in this world is nothing more than atoms vibrating to a certain frequency in order to exist, then does this mean that there may be other worlds existing outside of our frequency range?

According to studies, the human eye can only see roughly (some say more, some less) around 0.05% of the light spectrum. What we call visible light. This means there is roughly 99.95% that goes undetected by the human eye. So, with that knowledge, you have to ask: What could be going on in front of our very eyes every day that we simply cannot see?

When people claim to have seen a ghost (and I have experienced this several times), sometimes their report states that it appeared from nowhere or that it simply vanished right in front of their eyes. How is this possible? Nothing can just disappear in to thin air. Is it possible, however, that the figure that they have seen, for the briefest of moments, came in to the viewer's frequency range (visible light) and then "tuned out" of the frequency range, meaning that they are no longer visible to the human eye, but possibly still there? I would argue that this could very well be the case. An example I use when discussing this with people is that of radio stations. I'm sure that we have all, at one point, been driving along listening to a radio station (let's say Radio X) and all of a sudden Radio X is interrupted by Radio Y. For a brief moment, both stations exist as you struggle to hear which song is which before the station corrects itself and you're back to Radio X. All that has happened is your radio (frequency receiver) has briefly picked up two frequencies before returning to its original frequency. This could be what is happening when someone is witnessing the apparition of a ghost. To go a little deeper with this analogy, just because your frequency receiver/decoder (radio) is picking up Radio X, that doesn't mean that Radio Y no longer exists. Of course, it still exists, it is just on a different frequency to what you are currently tuned in to and so your radio cannot pick up that frequency. Now replace the word radio here with brain and you may understand what it is I am trying to say. Just because we cannot see anything outside of our frequency range, it doesn't mean that there is nothing existing there. Maybe, if you follow this theory, mediums or psychics have an ability to tune in to these frequencies, hence why they can communicate with whatever is living outside of our normal frequency range. Imagine having a radio that allowed you to listen to two stations at once. Now that would certainly be interesting.

It is this type of thinking that has pushed me to continue my investigations in to the world of the paranormal. Using different techniques, myself and the other crew members try to find ways of communicating with the spirit world, some with good results.

Throughout this book it is my intention to explain these experiments; why we use them, what they achieve and the resulting evidence, if any. There willl also be a few more ghost stories, both first hand and experiences from family and friends. Enjoy!

EMF Meter

Some people may know this device as a "K2". To describe this device simply, from a paranormal investigation standpoint, it is a small, handheld device that is used to measure electromagnetic fields (EMF for short). These devices are probably the most common piece of kit in any investigator's equipment box. Most people will also have seen it in use on paranormal TV shows.

On a day to day basis, these devices are used to diagnose any problems with things such as electrical wiring or faulty electrical goods, like a microwave. If there are issues, the EMF meter will flag up. Although you can purchase digital EMF meters, the most common ones will have a set of lights ranging from green to yellow to red, with red indicating the highest EMF fluctuation.

On a paranormal investigation, these devices are used to, supposedly, detect when a spirit is near or is interacting with the group. This would imply that whatever is interfering with the device has the capability to affect the electromagnetic field that is around us. A member of the crew will normally speak out to the spirits, encouraging them to come forward and interact with the device, making the lights change from green to red. It must be said that this does happen. I have seen, on multiple occasions, these devices begin to flash. Sometimes slowly and cautiously and other times the device has been flashing like crazy.

Now, it is possible to create a reaction on these devices with no spirits involved at all. Most of these devices are switched on using a large button in the middle of the device. Press it once to turn it on, press it again to turn it off. However, if you hold your finger on the button once switched on and keep it somewhere between on and switching off, the lights go crazy, acting as it would if a "spirit" was in close proximity. I just thought I would add this bit of information as I have seen it happen several times. For best results, with no help from a human hand, the device should be placed down on a table, a chair or the floor and it should be left alone, viewed from a distance.

One such example of an EMF meter being interacted with happened at the Ancient Ram Inn in Gloucester. The crew were split in to two teams, myself not involved with this particular part of the investigation, but I have been briefed by the crew as to what happened.

The crew and guests were located in one of the living areas where there is an old fireplace built in to one of the walls. They were all seated in a circle next to the fireplace calling out and waiting for a response. After a while, and with there being no response to the initial questions, they decided to switch on the EMF meters. They placed one device on a table that was located in the centre of the circle and one was placed on a vacant chair that formed part of the circle. Once both were in place, they began to call out again, but this time asking for the lights on the devices to be interacted with, hoping to see them change colour. It didn't take long for the device in the centre of the circle to begin flashing in reaction to the questions. At this point the lights were going up to orange, which is about midway. Once it had reached orange it would then return to green. This happened several times upon request. Now the crew asked for the same interaction to happen to the device placed on the chair. After a short while it responded, but only when the one in the centre of the circle had stopped. At this point they noticed the light changing on the chair was stronger, with it going all the way to red. With this in mind they moved the other device on to the same chair, also, to see if both could be interacted with at the same time. Now both devices were lighting up all the way to red and back down to green in synchronisation and only upon request. The team would ask for the lights to change and they would respond. After some time, they began to not respond and eventually the interaction stopped.

I heard this story from the crew involved at the end of the investigation, where we normally discuss our findings and thoughts. I found it a very interesting occurrence, mainly due to the lights being activated on command. When I hear such stories as this, where an EMF meter has been very active in a certain part of a location, my initial thoughts are to consider the electrical wiring of the house and whether there was any electrical equipment near the crew when conducting the experiment. It goes without saying that any of the above, and even mobile phones that aren't switched off or on flight mode, can greatly affect the results of an EMF meter, leading a person to believe it is being interacted with by a spirit. The building that was being investigated at the time is a very old building, almost derelict in parts. In fact, we were not allowed to step in parts of the building for health and safety reasons. The parts of the building that were wired up seemed to be fine; no exposed wires sticking out of the walls or dodgy looking fuse boxes. This, and the numerous "on command" responses, led me to believe that there was no electrical interference with the EMF meter.

The crew that were involved stated that it was almost like a child was playing with the devices, running between the two, as if it was playing some sort of game. Of course, this can't be substantiated, but I do find it very strange that the lights were acting as requested. If nothing was asked, they didn't respond. To me, this could possibly indicate an intelligent response. A reactive response, maybe. There are times when an EMF meter is lighting up but there doesn't seem to be any pattern to the reactions. When this happens, I tend to lean more towards the possibility of interference from an electrical source. However, when it responds as it did for the crew and guests at the Ancient Ram Inn, it gets a little more interesting and the possibilities of what could be causing the interaction become more obscure.

I feel that I must add here that I wondered around this building with my EMF meter in hand most of the night and not once did I get any reaction on the lights. Even when I was located in the area that this particular experience occurred, I didn't get a single reaction to my requests. Once the investigation had ended, I remember feeling a little disappointed with the evening and my personal experiences, but it seems there were other members of the crew who had experienced a very interactive night.

One important thing to remember here is that the EMF meter can be interfered with by mobile phones and other electrical equipment. With that in mind, it is important, when using an EMF meter during an investigation, that electrical equipment, such as mobile phones, are switched off or, at the very least, put on flight mode. This is one way to ensure your investigation isn't giving you false evidence.

As far as I am aware, there have been numerous studies in to the effects of EMF on us as humans. Some research in particular has focused on the effects that electromagnetic fields have on the human sleep cycle and the levels of melatonin produced by an individual. Melatonin is a hormone that is produced by your pineal gland (known to some spiritualists as the "third eye"). Melatonin, when released in to the blood stream, begins to make you feel tired and leaves you in need of sleep. The release of melatonin is regulated by light, with the pineal gland being inactive during the day. It is once night arrives, and with it darkness, that the melatonin levels begin to rise and the need for sleep shortly follows. Studies have suggested that the rise in EMF that now surrounds us all on a daily basis is beginning to have an effect on the human body. In a short space of time, we have surrounded ourselves with Wi-Fi, 3G, 4G, and at the time of writing this, the coming of 5G. These invisible frequencies may be having more of an effect on us than some may think. I know of people who began to suffer insomnia until they turned off their Wi-Fi and removed their phone from beside their bed when going to sleep. This seemed to help them immensely, and it does point towards the EMF being pulsed around their home as the culprit to their lack of sleep.

One investigation in America involved a person who was struggling to sleep in their new home. They would regularly wake up with the feeling of someone pressing down on their throat and chest, struggling to breathe, and had the sense that there was always someone in the room with them, watching them as they lay in their bed, trying to sleep. Their sense of paranoia within their new home had increased ten-fold over a short period of time and they became convinced that the house that they had recently moved in to was haunted. As most people do when they acquire a new home, this individual began work to improve the house. Part of this work included re-wiring the electrics to make it a safe home to live in. It was around the time that this work began that the "hauntings" started. As the work on the house continued, it was eventually noted that the re-wiring hadn't been done very well at all and, due to it still being unsafe, the wiring needed to be started over. Once this work had been completed and the wiring was now deemed safe, the "hauntings" immediately stopped. No longer did the individual feel a sense of paranoia when in the house. Nor did they struggle with sleep and wake with the sense of someone, or something, sitting on their chest. The investigation concluded that the "spirit" was nothing more than faulty wiring in the house, which had been flooding it with EMF and affecting the occupant in a negative way, making them feel like they were being watched and causing them many a sleepless night.

Had someone entered the house with an EMF meter, and not been aware of the faulty wiring, they would have no doubt seen huge interactions with the lights on their meter and possibly used it as evidence to back up the occupant's original fears that the house was indeed haunted.

Whilst there isn't any scientific evidence to suggest a spirit can interact with the electromagnetic fields that surround us, there is evidence of how everyday items that we use can. That being said, I have experienced EMF meters being active when, to my knowledge, there isn't anything in near proximity that could possibly be the cause for the interaction with the lights. As I mentioned previously, when carrying out an investigation, do make sure that any items that could interact with your equipment are either turned off or out of the way. This is one way of ensuring that any evidence you capture may just be paranormal.

Human Pendulum

I briefly explained this experiment at the start of the book, where I experienced, first hand, the effects that this can have on the individual that is involved.

The human pendulum is an experiment that really can divide the group that is involved in the investigation. Some will love it and will want to get involved, whilst others will simply opt to watch from the side lines and see what happens. I have come across some people who have flat out refused to participate in any way. I believe this to be because of the way the experiment requires a spirit to interact directly with the person and not a device of some kind, as with the EMF Meter. This direct interaction with a spirit, where there is a possibility of being touched or pushed, is a daunting prospect and I completely understand when anyone says that they do not wish to participate.

The crew will always ask for a volunteer here, which is where we normally see the divide in the group occur. It isn't very often that we will have a volunteer raise their hand and put themselves forward straight away. Sometimes we have guests who jump at the opportunity to participate, but when we struggle to get a volunteer, we try to explain that no harm will come to anyone and that they can leave the experiment at any time. If we ever do an investigation that is crew only then, because we all know the experiment well and what we can expect from the participation, we have no problems regarding volunteers, but when the public are involved, we have to be careful that we don't push someone in to doing it against their will.

Once we have someone willing to participate then the rest of the team will form a circle around the volunteer who will have two members of the crew with them; one a few steps in front of them and one a few steps behind. The reason for this positioning is purely for health and safety, making sure the person doesn't fall and hurt themselves.

Now that everything is in place, we then begin the experiment. A member of the crew will begin to relax the volunteer. It is important to stress here that the experiment does not, in any way, involve hypnosis. At least when we do it, anyway. We ask everyone to remain as quiet as possible. This allows the volunteer to be able to focus on the voice of our crew member. The volunteer is asked to lower their head and rest their chin on their chest and allow their arms to relax by their side. Then, as described in the prologue, the crew member begins to count down from ten, constantly making sure the volunteer is relaxed but is also aware enough to hear the crew member's voice.

Once the countdown has reached one, the crew member steps away from the volunteer and they begin to ask for a yes answer. It is at this point that we normally see the volunteer beginning to sway. It can be backwards, forwards or, on rare occurrences, sideways. This is where the two crew members become prepared to catch the volunteer should they sway too far and look like they are about to fall. Once satisfied that there has been a clear response to the question, they now ask for a no answer. What makes this experiment interesting to me is that this will almost always cause the volunteer to sway in the opposite direction than they did for a yes answer. Again, once satisfied that there is a clear distinction between the two answers, the crew member will begin to ask a series of questions and await the response by way of movement.

Having taken part in this, what was difficult to understand was how it really didn't feel like I was moving at all in response to the questions. I was told I was swaying backwards and forwards quite aggressively, yet I felt like I was standing completely still and up right. A large number of volunteers report the same feelings after they have participated. A feeling of calmness and stillness, yet to the people watching, they are swinging backwards and forwards, sometimes with extremity.

One of the best human pendulums that I have witnessed to date occurred in Drakelow Tunnels, in the very same room that I had my experience. The lady participating was a family friend who had joined us on the investigation along with my mum. As far as I am aware, she is a sceptic but does have an interest in anything paranormal. This is something that we seem to encounter a lot; people who don't believe but are interested in coming on events. I am not sure if it is to prove themselves right in their beliefs or even to prove themselves wrong and see if they experience something outside of their belief system. Despite being a sceptic, she was very nervous and stuck close to the group throughout the entire night. This is why I was so surprised when she put her hand up and volunteered to take part in the human pendulum. She had no idea what it was, no idea as to previous results (in that particular room) and it was her first investigation, let alone first time as a volunteer in an experiment of this kind.

Everything I have described so far relating to how this experiment is conducted happened here; we relaxed her, had two crew members, one stood in front and one stood behind and began to ask for a yes and no answer. The reactions were very minimal to start with and I remember thinking that it could have been her scepticism, or a strong will for nothing to influence her, that may be causing the lack of response to the questions being asked. Not long in to the experiment, however, she began to sway more wildly, often needing to be pushed back upright by the crew. This then progressed to even wilder movements, until eventually it resulted in her standing still, feet rooted to the floor, shaking as if she was having a seizure. This wasn't a nice thing to witness and was the first and only time it has happened on our investigations. At this point all of the crew asked the group members to take a step back and allow us to try and relax the volunteer. This is done by using a spiritual type of practise called "grounding". This involves placing our hands upon the shoulders or head of the person being affected and trying to draw the negative energy away and relax the person. In this particular instance it took a while, as she was being affected so badly.

Eventually, we opted to lead her from the room and she finally began to relax and come around. This was a very scary moment for everyone involved. The other guests were obviously worried for the safety of the volunteer, as were the crew. Once she was feeling more relaxed, she struggled to recall anything that had happened during the experiment but stated that she felt fine and was happy to continue. Although not identical to my reaction when participating in this experiment in the same room, it is very interesting when there are similar results from our experiments when conducted in the same area with different groups of people. It certainly helps to back up that there is indeed something strange occurring in these places.

Another human pendulum experiment that fascinated me was carried out during an investigation at my local pub. It was a location that I had been looking at investigating for a long time and it didn't disappoint. The main part of the pub can be dated back 400 plus years, along with evidence of Tudor brickwork found in the cellar, so there is a lot of history to the place.

When carrying out the human pendulum experiment, I asked a guest who had been coming across as very sceptical throughout the night to have a go and he agreed. Again, we had two people, one in front and one behind the volunteer, making sure he didn't fall or stumble. Once the volunteer was relaxed, I started to ask my questions. After several minutes I was beginning to consider wrapping the experiment up, as the volunteer was showing hardly any signs of movement or responses to the questions that I was asking him. This may have been down to his scepticism and his willingness to prove that spirits don't actually exist. Just before wrapping it up I decided to ask one last time for a yes answer. At this point I noticed the lady who was stood in front of the volunteer began to rock backwards, quite noticeably. When seeing this I asked for a no answer and watched her change direction very abruptly and begin to rock forwards. It was here that I realised that I had been focusing on the wrong person for the answers to my questions. It must be said that I have never encountered a human pendulum experiment where the person who becomes affected and begins answering the questions that are being asked is not the person who volunteered. It was a very intriguing situation to see. I placed my hand on the original volunteer and asked him to open his eyes and be sure that the new "volunteer" didn't stumble. I quickly placed a person behind her and continued to ask my questions. Over the course of the next five minutes or so, the new participant slowly began to hunch up, with her arms held out in front of her and her palms facing upwards. We quickly established that the spirit that seemed to be affecting her had previously owned the pub and she was known to a few of the guests, who then proceeded to ask questions. After several minutes of questioning, the participant began to look extremely uncomfortable. When this happens, which is quite common, we always try to wrap the experiment up as quickly as possible so as not to cause any more distress than is necessary for both the volunteer and the guests. I placed my hand on her shoulder and I began to bring her around. Once she was out of the experiment, she pointed out that she had absolutely no awareness of her movements, of which the whole group had witnessed. She said that she was aware of the questions being asked but she was not aware of her stance and awkward positioning. What interested me the most was that she had never met, heard of or knew the spirit that had supposedly been interacting with her. Yet she had answered all of the questions correctly, some quite personal to the friendships that had existed between the spirit and the guests asking the questions.

Whilst I always enjoy the human pendulum experiment and watching the volunteers react how they do, I do often wonder how many of the reactions are springing from the subconscious of the volunteer. Please don't think that I am calling all volunteers liars, here. Remember, I had a very strange experience of my own when taking part in this and I certainly didn't fake any of it, as I believe the volunteers mentioned above didn't either. What I mean to say is; could it be possible that the volunteer is answering the questions unconsciously, without really knowing what they are doing?

Some guests will attend our investigations so intent on finding evidence and backing up their beliefs, that they will draw "evidence" out of anything that they can. In situations like this, the slightest noise is always credited to a spirit. The truth is, however, more often than not it is simply someone's stomach grumbling at 10:30pm or someone shifting their tired, aching feet at 1:00am. Again, I am not saying that they come and fake events to justify their beliefs, just that they find their beliefs in every little thing that occurs on an investigation. So, with that in mind, I do believe it is possible that the human pendulum could utilise this and cause the volunteer to sway in answer to the questions being asked, not because they are being influenced by a spirit, but because they may want it so badly that they answer the questions themselves, without really knowing. Of course, the above way of thinking could be applied across the board when it comes to paranormal investigations. People will always see what they want to see. As a team who invite paying guests on to investigations, it is sometimes best to let them hold on to what they are experiencing, as it may be important to that person. For example, if they have recently lost a loved one then they may be looking for signs in anything they see or hear. If this helps them feel at peace, then I am more than happy to let it happen. However, as a crew, our values lie with trying to find definitive evidence and ruling out any possibility that it is something not paranormal before we can even begin to consider that it is paranormal activity that we are encountering.

Spirit Walkthrough

I thought I would include this experiment as part of the human pendulum chapter, as it is very much the same except for the number of participants and the questions that are asked.

This experiment usually takes four volunteers, but can be increased or decreased in numbers, who are then asked to stand in a line. Sometimes we ask for them to be facing the same way and other times we ask for them to face each other. Either way we leave a good few feet of space between each one, so that the crew members can stand there for their safety, as with the human pendulum. Once everyone is in place, we then line any of the remaining crew members or guests either side of the volunteers so that they can see any movement or swaying that may occur once the experiment begins.

Once we are ready to begin, a crew member relaxes the volunteers exactly the same way as with the human pendulum. Once they are relaxed and the count down from ten to one has finished, the crew member in charge will make their way to the end of the line of volunteers and begin to ask the spirits to make their way to the source of the voice. At this point, we usually begin to see movement from at least one of the volunteers. They continue to ask for a minute or so more and then move to the other end to repeat the process. Again, the volunteers usually begin to sway towards to the voice. It must be said, though, that not all volunteers react as strongly as others, and some don't react at all. Occasionally, the crew member will stand at the side of the line and ask for the spirits to move towards their voice, just to see if the volunteers will sway sideways. This does happen, but very rarely. On some occasions, the crew member will ask for a yes and no answer, like the human pendulum, and then continue asking questions. The issue with this line of questioning for this particular experiment is that not all of the volunteers will answer yes by swaying the same way. Of course, the sceptical side of me then sees the experiment as nothing more than an act of subconscious when answering the questions. I have had people theorise that maybe there is more than one spirit interacting with the volunteers and that is why the answers are different person to person. Whilst this could very well be a possibility, I truly believe that it is more related to the subconscious.

Once the crew member is happy that they have got all that they can from the experiment, they then begin to count from one to ten and tell the volunteers to lift their heads and move around. Sometimes, as with the human pendulum, volunteers will express how they had felt a pulling or tugging on their limbs or clothing.

One spirit walkthrough that really sticks out in my mind happened at Smethwick Swimming Baths. We had decided to do the walkthrough in the sauna, a decision I soon regretted due to the heat. Even in the middle of the night, with the sauna being inactive, I remember that it was ridiculously warm, as swimming baths always are. We gathered together our volunteers and lined them up down the middle of the sauna, with the remaining guests and crew down each side. Some were relaxing on the reclining sun beds that were in there, some were a little more tense. It was rather nice but too long on there and I would have been fast asleep. We began to ask the usual questions, looking for a response. In this particular experiment, I was on the side, not standing next to a volunteer. I find this gives a different perspective altogether. When you are in front or behind a volunteer, it is difficult to see the full range of movement that is occurring in response to the questions. Obviously, you know they are moving because you are the one preventing them from falling over and pushing them back up in to a straight position. Standing on the side, however, allows the full range of movement to be seen. It also allows you to be able to relax as you aren't primarily responsible for the safety of the volunteer, so there is a little pressure taken off, allowing for the full experience of the experiment.

The questions being asked and the responses from the volunteers were pretty standard, as far as a spirit walkthrough goes. One lady in particular seemed to be affected more so than the other volunteers. Her movements were much more violent and the crew members near her were signalling so. I remember moving down towards that end of the room to keep a closer eye on her and give the crew members a little help should they have needed it. After a few minutes she began to move even more violently and began to cry. We halted the experiment and shifted our attention on to her as she seemed very distressed. As with the human pendulum, we all began trying to "ground" her. In this instance, it didn't work as well as we would have liked and she continued to be distressed and very confused. When she finally spoke, it was very random and didn't really make much sense to any of us. We began to ask her questions, just to see if she was coherent and understood what was going on. At this point we realised that she didn't seem to be herself. When we asked her how she had got to the venue (she had travelled by car with her two daughters), she replied that she had arrived by horse and cart. We then asked if she could tell us what year it was and she answered 1873. Of course, at this point, everyone begins to think that she is possessed and so the panic that people are feeling becomes heightened. As a crew we decided to remove her from the area that we were situated in and some of the crew members took the lady outside, where they continued trying to relax her and bring her around from the confused state that she was in. For a while, she continued to belicve she had arrived on horseback with her husband, when in fact she had arrived by car with her two daughters. Eventually she came around and relaxed considerably enough to re-join the investigation.

As with the human pendulum, I have to question how much of the movement involved here is down to spirits interacting with the volunteers and how much is down to the volunteers allowing their subconscious or their beliefs to influence their movements. The difference between these two experiments is the purpose. The human pendulum is used to ascertain purposefully asked questions to which a yes or no can be answered. Are you male? Are you happy with us being here? Sometimes, the research that the crew have carried out on the location will have given us an insight to the history or certain events involving certain people. It is this research that often dictates the questions that we ask. Although the volunteer may also know the history, it may not be the case, which means if they answer the questions in such a way that coincide with what we know through our research, then it opens up the possibility that it may very well be a spirit influencing the answers. However, the spirit walkthrough, on most occasions, asks the spirits to move towards a voice. If the volunteers are allowing their subconscious to control their answers, then it is a case of simply moving your body towards the voice that is speaking. This, of course, could be rectified by putting headphones on the volunteers to prevent them from hearing the voice or questions being asked. If the volunteers can't hear what is being said, yet still move towards the voice or answer the questions correctly, then this could very well eliminate the subconscious theory and open up the possibility that the interaction is actually with a spirit.

However, whilst these experiments are good to watch, and they are very involving for the guests, I believe it leaves too much to the subconscious for it to be conclusive that spirits are interacting with the volunteers at all times.

Psychic Handwriting

Also known as automatic handwriting, this experiment is carried out on very rare occasions. On a personal level I am glad, as I am not the biggest fan of this experiment. With that being said, it is easy enough to carry out; some paper, some pencils, tables and chairs and eye masks to cover the eyes and you are ready to go.

Automatic handwriting has been practised for centuries throughout different cultures. There have even been some famous cases of automatic handwriting being carried out. One of these includes the author, Charles Dickens. When he died in 1870, as is the case with most authors, he had some unfinished work. Three years after his death, a printer named Thomas P James spoke publicly about how he had contacted the spirit of Charles Dickens and that the now dead author was happy to use Thomas as a writing vessel so that he could finally complete one of his unfinished books, "The Mystery of Edwin Drood". Thomas would sit and supposedly channel Charles Dickens as he wrote page after page and completed the book.

The premise behind the experiment on a paranormal investigation is for a person to be blindfolded, relaxed and to be holding a pencil to paper, allowing spirits to use the person as a vessel through which they can write any messages they should have from the afterlife. Of course, the reason for the blindfold is to prevent the person participating in the experiment being able to see what they are writing. Essentially, it is so they don't lie or cheat. We also tend to ask our participants to use their weaker hand when "writing". Again, this is to prevent any fraudulent attempts. It is much easier to write with your preferred hand, even when blindfolded.

Once we have the guests sat at the tables, along with any crew willing to participate, we explain the experiment. What we are hoping to achieve here is for the writer to be fully relaxed and to let go of any conscious thoughts. This is a very difficult task to accomplish but if anyone is familiar with meditation it really does help where this experiment is concerned. Once blindfolded, we ask them to put pencil to paper and we then await any results. Some people claim that they can feel their hand being pulled or moved. When this happens, we encourage them to let it happen naturally and to not offer any resistance. There are always a couple of crew members walking around the tables, ensuring that everyone is fine and that no one is cheating, such as pulling up their blindfold whilst writing. This may sound very untrustworthy, but we have had people on events who are there for a laugh and a giggle. On the whole, we don't mind this, as we believe that good energy and good vibrations help when it comes to encountering an active location. However, we don't wish it to disturb any experiments and potentially ruin it for any other guests.

I have participated in this experiment a few times now and I have never really felt that my hand was being guided. In fact, I even fell asleep at one point! The blindfold and the relaxation were just too much for me at 1:00am.

Regarding any results, we have had a few instances where people have spelt out names or words, but nothing of great significance. Most people will have drawn patterns of some kind. I have seen these patterns attempted to be explained as something or other but I just can't bring myself to see any significance behind them. I feel there really is too much potential for the subconscious to become involved here. Not only the subconscious, either. If someone really wishes to confirm their beliefs, or maybe someone is just being a little mischievous as mentioned above, I feel that this experiment is too easy to cheat on. I have tried this myself. I had my blindfold on and, even with my weaker hand, managed to spell a name or two. It is just too simple.

At one investigation I decided to put this to the test. I had a close friend accompany me on this particular investigation and throughout the day that we had spent together and the night that we were investigating I had kept dropping the same name in to conversation. Not so that he would notice I was up to something, but strategically placed in to our conversations here and there. Eventually, the time came for us to carry out the automatic handwriting experiment. My friend sat at the table alongside the other guests and placed his blindfold over his eyes. He picked up the pencil with his weak hand and sat waiting for any sign of activity. We normally carry out this experiment over the course of ten minutes or so. This helps prevent guests getting bored, where they are likely to either begin doodling or, as I did, fall asleep. Around the five-minute mark I happened to be walking past where my friend was sat and noticed there was some scrawling on his piece of paper. I was anxious to see what it said but waited until the experiment had come to an end. Eventually, we called time on the experiment and the guests lifted their blindfolds and began chatting amongst themselves about what they had, or hadn't, written in their relaxed state. I headed over to my friend to see what they had scribbled. Sure enough, he had written, in very rough handwriting, the name that I had been dropping in to our conversations throughout the day. Whilst I was a little shocked that it had worked, it did help deepen my belief that this experiment is just too easy to either fake or subconsciously manipulate.

Now, at this point, some people may be questioning where I stand on the paranormal. In fact, I remember one of my first investigations I was called a sceptic. This was because I was trying to debunk everything and explain it using natural occurrences. This really couldn't be further from the truth. I have had some very strange and vivid experiences during my time as an investigator and even outside of the group, too. Too much has happened for me to not believe there is something going on. With that being said, I believe that the best way to approach an investigation is by doing so with a clear, unbiased view. Believe me, I would like more than anyone to be able to show definitive proof of a spirit and that is why I do what I do, but there has to be a clear, unbiased approach when conducting investigations. If there is a sound that seems like it could be someone shuffling their feet, then the chances are that it probably is someone shuffling their feet. My rule of thumb is to always rule out what it isn't before you can decide what it is. Some people, and I speak of fellow investigators here, as well as guests, are far too quick to jump to the paranormal conclusion without giving a second thought in to what else it could be. So, I take this approach in to every investigation and experiment I do, both individually and as a group. As for the automatic handwriting, I feel it leaves too much to the person conducting the experiment for it to possibly be paranormal.

Spirit Board

Almost everyone will have heard of this experiment, although most probably by its other name, the Ouija Board. This is, without doubt, the most popular way of trying to contact spirits. Like with most experiments, it is easy enough to set up and conduct. Most people who carry out this activity will own a board themselves but I have seen makeshift ones in use. I have seen letters cut out of paper and made in to a circle with the glass in the middle and it still worked. There are times that we seem to be getting no response on the board so we opt to use just the glass. We ask for a yes and no answer and once the different moving patterns are figured out, usually a straight line and a circle, we proceed with asking the questions. Again, this has had large success. This is what I always tell people who see a spirit board as evil and as a way for "demons" to access this world. The board itself is nothing more than wood with some letters and numbers on. If a spirit wishes to communicate, they will communicate by any means. That doesn't make the board itself evil.

The way this experiment works, if you didn't already know, is by taking a glass (turned upside down) or a shaped piece of wood or plastic known as a planchette, placing fingers on the object and allowing the spirit to guide it around the board, choosing letters along the way in order to spell their message. The spirit does this by supposedly using the energy of the participants.

Most boards will contain a similar layout; letters from A to Z, a Hello and Goodbye, a Yes and No and numbers from 1 to 10. This tends to give the spirit everything they should need in order to make contact with the living.

The term Ouija is actually from a games manufacturer back when the board was used as little more than a parlour type game. My great aunty had one that the family used to play with at family occasions, such as Christmas. The word itself is a combination of the French and German words for "yes".

On investigations we tend to have a lot of guests who see the spirit board as something that is evil and not to be messed with. Unfortunately, in my opinion, a lot of the bad feelings towards it are down to horror films where bad things occur as a result of messing around with a board. For something that effectively started out as a game, it really has gained a bad reputation over time. Personally, I have never had a bad experience whilst conducting this experiment. Not bad in the sense of evil and being afraid, anyway. I have a board in my house, although I know of people who even refuse to have one in their home as it can be seen as a portal for dark spirits to come and go. When we conduct this experiment on an investigation, whether with guests or not, we always "open" and "close" the board. What this entails is placing your hands upon the board and asking that only spirits with honest, truthful intentions and love come forward and so on. When "closing" the board, hands are again placed on the board and we ask that spirits now cease to use the board and that they leave us alone when we leave and so on. It may sound like I am being vague here and that is because I am. It really is down to whoever is controlling the experiment and what they wish to say when starting and ending the session, so there isn't really a strict quote that needs to be spoken.

Once our board is "open" and the glass is in place at the centre of the board, we ask for volunteers who wish to participate. As I have already mentioned, we get a lot of people who flat out refuse to participate. We have even had people who don't want to be in the same room or area that we are conducting the experiment, such is their bad feelings towards using a board. Through experience, the board tends to work when you have more than two participants. I am not sure why this is, but it could be down to the energy required to move the glass, if that is how the glass is moved.

We now ask for our volunteers to place a finger on the top of the upturned glass. Personally, I tend to use my little finger placed upside down, and I encourage others to do so, too. The reason for this is it is much harder to control the glass yourself when pushing with the little finger, particularly when it is nail down on the glass. It is just another way I try to limit the "cheating" during an experiment.

When all of the fingers are in place, we "warm up" the board. This is done by rotating the glass around the board in a clockwise direction.

What I find good about doing this is when people are pushing the glass around the board you really can tell. Sometimes the glass falls over during this part as the pressure exerted by the volunteers to push the glass around causes it to fall.

Once "warmed up" we then begin to show the spirits how the board works. We move the glass around the letters, numbers and answers (yes, no etc.) to show them how they can respond to us. One of the reasons we do this is because we may be interacting with a spirit who is illiterate. If we are communicating with a spirit from the 19th century or earlier, it could very well be the case that they couldn't read or write when they were alive, so asking them to spell their name or communicate by way of spelling may not work. There is also the possibility that the spirit we are communicating with could be a child, in which case they may not be able to read or write, either.

At this point we now begin to ask questions. If we have guests participating, then we always allow them to lead the experiment. Whilst some people may participate by placing their finger on the glass, they may not necessarily be comfortable with speaking out. One thing we have found is that there have been times when someone has been asking questions yet we have had no response, but the second someone else begins to speak the glass begins to move. This could be because the spirit prefers this person or maybe they have an affinity towards males or females in particular. We have had instances where the board would not work when a male was speaking or participating. Once it was an all-female experiment, it started to interact and vice versa.

If we do happen to get any response to our questions, the time it takes to move really can vary. Sometimes we can feel the glass moving like an energy is building up within the glass itself but it fails to actually move across the board. There are times where the glass moves almost instantly, before any questions are asked and with a force that has taken us by surprise. Other times it seems to move very slowly. We have had responses where answers have been given clearly and quickly and other times the glass just roams around the board, not really making any sense to the participants. This could be a spirit playing around and having fun or maybe, as I mentioned before, a spirit who doesn't understand how to put the letters together.

We have had numerous experiences on the board that have left a particular mark on me and I will go in to a couple in greater detail.

Drakelow Tunnels Spirit Board

We quite often use the board down in Drakelow
Tunnels as we almost always get a great response, in
one area in particular. On several different
occasions, with different guests participating in the
activity, we have had the same name and the same
answers come through. What we do as a group is to
collate data from each investigation as it allows us to
trace similarities between investigations. For
example, in the same location there is a room known
as the Key Room, where the security guards were
based along with the keys for certain areas, hence
the name. We usually conduct a calling out session
in this room, with the group stood in a circle. On
numerous occasions, with different groups in
attendance, we have had the exact same claim of
what feels like a small animal, such as a cat or dog,
running between people's legs. I find it really
interesting when multiple claims from different
people on different occasions all share the same
experience. In this instance, it could possibly be a
guard dog used when the location was running daily.
Just as above, I find it strange that different people
can participate in the board experiment yet come out
with the exact same answers as a previous group.

One incident, however, really stands out to
me in Drakelow. As usual, we had set up the board
and gone through all of the pre-experiment rituals
that I have already explained earlier in this chapter.
Almost straight away we started to have activity
with the glass moving. We asked several questions,

one of them being "are you with anyone tonight?".
The glass, with a lot of force and speed, shot over to
where a young lady was stood. Of course, she
looked scared and hesitant to continue. We urged
her to carry on and, if she could, ask some questions
herself to see if she could ascertain who it could
possibly be that was interacting with us and seemed
to know her. The first thing she asked for was the
glass to spell her name. It did. At this point I asked
if she could remove her finger from the glass but
continue to ask the questions. The reason for this is I
wanted to make sure she wasn't influencing the
glass herself in anyway, be that subconsciously or
on purpose. She then asked a series of questions
such as date of birth, sisters name and so on. The
glass answered each of her questions correctly and
with no hesitation. With further questioning it
transpired that the spirit communicating with us was
related to this lady but from a previous life. We
eventually ended the experiment and the lady,
visibly shook up, left the investigation not long
after.

Smethwick Baths Spirit Board

Smethwick Baths is an absolute stand out location for me. One thing I will add here is that I have found that locations that look like they are haunted tend to not be as active as locations that you may, at first, think will be inactive. Another thing I have noticed is that if a location has been investigated regularly over some time by different groups and people, then it seems that the activity can diminish over time. Likewise, if a location hasn't been investigated before, or has only been investigated a handful of times, then the activity tends to be higher. A reason for this could be energy levels. If you follow the theory that spirits either are energy or use energy to interact with us, then it could be that by over investigating a location could lead to the spirits simply be tired or lacking the energy to interact. It could also mean that they are possibly just bored of interacting with people who are insistent on them "showing themselves". A location that has been investigated less regularly could contain spirits who still have energy to use. Another concept to think about is that if a location has never been investigated before, the spirits could be desperate to communicate with anyone looking to do so, but could also be hesitant and not really understand what is being asked of them or what is going on.

This location, for example, is investigated less regularly than others in the area and is a fully functioning swimming baths. That being said, it was one of the most active locations I have investigated to date. Not only was this my first investigation as an official member of the team, but it is the location where I had several experiences that will stay with me for a long time. One such experience involved me and another team member patrolling a corridor. The rest of the crew and guests were in a room somewhere, not far away. We had decided to hang around in this corridor as it felt like it could be active. It is difficult to explain how we get a feeling for a place or area potentially being active. I always put it down to energy and the vibrations that I am picking up. Sometimes I can know straight away if a location is going to be active or if it is going to be a long night. Within minutes of being in this corridor we heard a cough, almost a clearing of the throat like sound. It sounded like it had come from a female. We both looked at each other in shock before I ran down the corridor trying to find out where the noise had come from and to see if I could locate a lady who maybe had left the group. At the end of the corridor where the noise had emanated from was a large boiler type room with no way in or out besides the corridor I had just run down. So, if there had have been a living person responsible for the cough then they would have had nowhere to go besides back past us, and we certainly saw no living person in the corridor.

On my way back up the corridor, right in my ear, there was a tuneful whistle. Straight away I stopped walking, looking at my fellow crew member to see if he had heard it, too. He stated that he had.

This, combined with the cough, left me quite shaken.

Eventually, the rest of the crew and guests arrived back in the corridor. Because of the activity we encouraged some people to participate in doing a spirit board experiment. We set it up on the windowsill and several people had their fingers on the glass. The glass moved but very weakly. After a while everyone decided to move on, with the exception of the two of us who had stayed previously and one guest. We decided to continue using the board to see what results we could get. After several answers the guest thought that maybe it was his dad trying to communicate with him. I asked the guest if he would mind taking his finger off the glass but continue to ask questions, just as I had done with the lady in the previous example. He started to ask questions such as eldest child's name, name of his mum, how his dad had died, what street did they grow up on and so on. Just like the above example in Drakelow Tunnels, the glass answered every single question correctly and left the guest in tears. We eventually decided to end the board session and, having spoken to the guest shortly after, he was very happy that he had supposedly spoken to his dad, stating that his main purpose for coming along was just that. This makes me happy that, even if it wasn't his dad communicating with us, the guest went home a little more at peace than when he arrived.

What I find so interesting about these two examples, and others that I have experienced, is how the answers can be given so accurately even when the only person who could possibly know the answers no longer has any form of control over the movement of the glass. Myself and the other crew member participating in the board at Smethwick Baths didn't know the guest at all, yet, with our fingers on the glass, we seemingly answered every question that he asked correctly.

Despite all of this, I do have my reservations about the spirit board experiment. There is every possibility that the glass could be moved by a participant either on purpose or subconsciously. As with experiments such as the human pendulum, the participant may want an answer so badly that they create their own answers.

However, to question my questions, is it possible for one person to influence the glass when there are several other people also participating? If, for example, I wished to move the glass to the letter A but another participant wished to moved it to the letter T, what would happen? There would surely be some kind of subconscious struggle going on between the two of us and the glass would make no sense. Whenever we spell out a name, does that mean that every single participant wishes to spell out that exact name at the same time, either consciously or subconsciously? Surely the odds of this are very unlikely. Also, how do you explain different sets of groups getting the exact same answers in the same location on different investigations?

Hopefully, by now, you will see that I look at paranormal investigations with an open, yet slightly sceptical, mind. The spirit board, however, really does have me torn both ways. I can completely understand the devout sceptic where this experiment is concerned, but I have had far too many first hand experiences with this to be completely doubtful of its validity.

Spirit Box

The spirit box, also knows as a ghost box, is a really fascinating piece of equipment to be used on an investigation. A spirit box is nothing more than a radio that has the ability to scan through frequencies. The difference is, a normal radio will stop once it reaches a station, whereas a spirit box has that feature disabled and so keeps scanning through the frequencies. As a result, what you get is each available frequency being audible for a fraction of a second before moving to the next available frequency and so on. The idea behind this piece of equipment is to allow the spirit a chance to communicate with the investigators using a mixture of white noise, static and the words being captured for a brief moment on each frequency. This interests me because of the theory I explained at the start of the book, where I believe that spirits may be operating on different frequencies.

There arc many different types of spirit boxes available to buy, but as I have mentioned above, they are simply radios with the ability to scan frequencies with the stop function removed. With this in mind, I am sure it would be easy enough to create your own if you are technologically savvy. Some come with built in speakers and some have the ability to plug in an external speaker, should you require it to be louder. Almost all of them will have the ability to scan FM and AM frequencies and will "sweep" through them, creating the white noise effect. Again, most available devices will allow the "sweep" speed to be adjusted for faster or slower speeds. I know of people who prefer the slower speed as it allows time to capture potential words, yet others find it easier to detect apparent words when the device is moving through the frequencies much faster. As with most investigative techniques, it is each to their own and whatever works best for the individual or group conducting the investigation.

As with the EMF meter, this experiment is pretty simple to conduct; place the spirit box on a table (or other solid surface) and gather around so that everyone can hear it clearly, which is best achieved by circling the device, and begin calling out and asking questions. As the frequencies are being swept through, you may begin to hear answers to the questions you are asking.

As always, I bring a very sceptical mind to this experiment. However, before I go in to my scepticism, I would like to document one of my spirit box sessions that occurred with my brother.

When my nan passed away, as most families do on these occasions, we gathered together. In this instance it was at my parents' home. Whilst we were all together my grandad asked me and my brother if we would go down to his house and put all of the furniture back where it belonged. At the time, the bed was downstairs and, to make room for the bed, the table had been taken upstairs. Obviously, we agreed and we drove the short distance. Once inside the house we set about re-arranging the furniture. When it was all done and we were ready to leave, my brother asked if I would be interested in doing a quick spirit box session. Initially, this struck me as odd because my brother doesn't really show much of an interest in this kind of thing. I remembered that I had the device in my car so agreed, but made sure that we would both not tell our grandad what we were doing, for fear of upsetting him. We set it up and set about asking questions in the living room. What happened next really did leave me shocked and in a state of both confusion and sadness. To be honest, it also scared me a little.

We started by asking the simple questions such as "Nan, are you there?" We had the odd response as it was sweeping through the frequencies that sounded like a yes, but I thought that was too simple, so I asked further questions. I said that grandad was up our parents' house and that he would be back later. When I said this, we had the response of "Raymond". This is my grandad's name. This response piqued my interest as I found the odds slim that we would scan across a station saying Raymond at the exact time I mentioned my grandad. I remember confirming the response and saying "Yes, Raymond. He is at dad's house but will be back later." Upon saying this we were hit with two names back to back; "Adrian… Kieran…" Adrian is my dad's name and, obviously, Kieran is my own name. Now I definitely took an interest in what was going on. To have Raymond, Adrian and Kieran all in quick succession was, I believe, almost impossible. To add to the amazement we were both feeling, the name Kieran was said as "Kirran", which is exactly how my nan would say my name.

At this point we were both in shock at the answers we had received, so we stopped asking questions for a brief moment. During this time the device kept on scanning the frequencies and it sounded like a conversation was happening. My brother asked, "Who are you talking to, nan?" We didn't get a response to the question but what we did get was, "They're my grandchildren." At the time, with it sounding like there was a conversation happening, I remember saying to my brother that I felt she was talking to people about us. Again, I found it strange that we would get that phrase when it was indeed her grandchildren talking to her. Also, for any of you who are familiar with the use of a spirit box, it is strange to get such a lengthy phrase, due to the short time the frequencies are available before the scanner moves on. Normally, it is expected to just hear one-word answers, occasionally two. We then asked if she was in pain anymore and she replied with a simple "No". We told her that we were glad and we asked her where she was. She answered this question with the word "Terrifying" and we both looked at each other before my brother asked her to tell us what was terrifying. At this point we were both visibly upset. For a short while we didn't get an answer and the device itself went very quiet. I remember thinking that maybe it had broken or the batteries were running low but then it kicked in again with a few seconds of static and white noise before it eventually said the word "God". This is where I drew the line and left the house. My brother continued and said that he had been told to go upstairs to the bedroom but the session fizzled out and he eventually came outside to where I was stood, still shaking. The whole of this experience had us both upset, happy and scared but hearing that "God" was "Terrifying" really shook me up. Some people may find it strange that I investigate ghosts and spiritual activity but don't believe in god, but it is true. So, for a non-believer to apparently hear their nan, who has recently passed away, describe God as terrifying left quite the mark on me.

I eventually told my dad what had happened and he seemed fine about what we had done but told me never to tell my grandad about it. When I look back at the session now and think about the conversation that seemed to be going on, I like to think that she was in some kind of waiting room, waiting to pass over. She had only died roughly eight hours before and I think she was terrified because she didn't really understand where she was or what was going on.

Now, let's look at the spirit box, and my personal experience, from a sceptical point of view. Regarding my personal experience, I am glad my brother was there with me and we can both back each other up with what we believed we had heard on that day. However, it is possible that we only really heard what we wanted to hear. Yes, it is strange that we both seemed to hear the same things, but could we have just been leading each other along in our experience? As it is a personal experience, I can tell you that my brother and I were both feeling emotionally raw at the point of the spirit box session. We had just lost our nan and were both upset. With this in mind I believe it is possible for our emotions and our subconscious to create the answers we wanted. It is a weird one for me as I know that we definitely heard what I have transcribed above but, with the way a spirit box works, it is possible to get the answers that you so desire out of the white noise and jumbled up words the device creates when scanning through the frequencies.

Many times, on an investigation, we have had several people all hearing different interpretations of the words coming out of the device. A good example is where numbers are involved. Quite often someone will ask if a spirit can tell us how many other spirits are with us at that particular time, and we always seem to have people hearing different numbers. Some might say they heard six whilst others, hearing the same word, will say it was three. On the face of it, these words, when spoken, don't sound anything alike at all. However, when the words are coming through a device mixed with static and white noise, it can be difficult to differentiate between words. This can lead to individuals hearing exactly what they want to hear.

For me the spirit box is an interesting device and can lead to some very intriguing results. My only advice would be that this experiment should be approached with the knowledge that what you believe you are hearing may not be what is actually being said. This is known as *pareidolia*. This is a phenomenon where people may believe they are recognising words or patterns where there are, in fact, none at all. A great example of this is the ability we have to recognise faces everywhere. How often do you see a pattern in some woodwork or a cloud in the sky and your brain tells you it "looks" like a face? Although it looks like a face, it obviously isn't. This kind of phenomena could definitely play a part, not only in experiments involving a spirit box, but also paranormal investigations altogether. This really is worth keeping in mind when conducting any experiment.

Scrying

Scrying has been used for hundreds of years as a way of seeing things that seemingly exist within another realm, visions, messages or spirits. Throughout the ages, scrying has been used by clairvoyants, fortune tellers, mediums and, most recently, paranormal investigators. Most paranormal investigative teams will carry out their scrying experiment by using a reflective surface, which is usually a mirror. As most investigations are carried out in the dark, a torch is shone so that the person taking part in the experiment can see themselves in the mirror. Historically, people have used scrying in many different forms. These have included; the classic crystal ball, made famous by fortune tellers, especially when depicted in films and the media, making sense of cloud shapes, using the smoke emanating from a fire or even just staring in to the darkness waiting for a sign or a message. Some people even conduct "eyelid scrying", where an individual will simply close their eyes and use the inside of their eyelids as a means of seeing messages or visions. This is something I have tried myself when trying to meditate. I say trying because it is something that I really do need to work on in order to perfect. With my eyes closed, I often see shapes and blurred images. Because of this I did a little bit of research in to what this could be. From what I understand, it is just to do with phosphenes, which are the patterns and visual sensations that we see when we close our eyes. These are caused when the retina continues to work as it does when the eye is open, producing electrical charges needed to process all of the information we see. However, because the eyes are closed, we now see these phosphenes against our eyelids.

As far as paranormal investigators go, as mentioned above, the most used form of scrying is by way of using a mirror, or other reflective surface. This experiment is cheap enough to carry out, as most venues that are investigated will have a mirror of some sorts, but most crews will also have one or two smaller mirrors in with their kit. Once positioned in front of a mirror, a torch is shone and the scrying session can begin. We tend to have two people participating in the scrying itself. with the other members of the group gathered around to see if they can see anything strange happening within the reflection. A scrying session can last as long as the participant or the group are willing to carry on, but it usually does last around five minutes or so. Due to the experiment not really being an active one for all group members, I feel that guests can get a little bored when this is happening. During the short experiment, the individual who is looking in to the mirror may begin to see their face change shape, or take on new features that were previously not there. Some people even claim that their face has taken on features of the opposite sex. Whilst the participant is noticing changes in their reflection, the people around them who are watching the experiment quite often claim to see changes in the reflection, too. Similar to what the individual participating may see, there have been claims of a "person" stood next to the reflection but not physically in the room, claims of flashing lights in the reflection and also claims of the reflection looking absolutely nothing like the volunteer who is stood in front of the mirror.

One experiment that we carried out using scrying had the participant break down in a flood of tears. She claimed that she could see herself changing in to an older lady in the reflection and that she was beginning to feel emotions that were being passed on to her from the spirit she was supposedly morphing in to in the mirror. She claimed she had begun to feel a huge sense of loss and a sadness that she was no longer in this world or that she could no longer be with her friends and family. Interestingly, some of the people within the group who were watching the reflection in the mirror also claimed that they could see her face changing and morphing in to that of an older lady. One person even said that they could see a bonnet on the head of the reflection.

Whilst I enjoy a bit of scrying here and there, I do find that it can drag on a little bit as an experiment when there is a group of people involved. My reason for saying this is that for the person actually staring in to the mirror, it can be quite fun and interesting to see if there are any changes to their appearance or the surroundings contained within the reflection. However, for the rest of the group, it can be a struggle at times to even see the mirror, especially if it is a little on the small side. Usually, the group tend to get restless and bored if this particular experiment drags on for too long, which I can completely understand. With that in mind, I tend to encourage the scrying section of an investigation whilst there are other activities for the group to be doing. For example, if we split in to smaller numbers to cover the venue or site, then I may conduct a small scrying session, as the smaller numbers mean that the people can feel more involved with the experiment, even if they aren't the individual staring in to the mirror.

Whilst scrying remains quite a popular experiment within the paranormal investigative circuit, I really do have my reservations about it. For me, pareidolia has the potential to play a huge part with this experiment. Staring in to a mirror for a prolonged period of time with no light source other than a torch is, in my opinion, going to cause the participant, and others watching, to see shapes, shadows and images that may not be there. For example, shining a torch beneath your face will highlight certain lines and features in the reflection, causing a nose to look distorted or eyes to look different. For those that are watching the experiment being conducted from behind, looking in to the mirror from different angles, with only the torch to show them the reflection, will no doubt cause some trickery in the viewers mind. In my opinion, there is far too much possibility that the person engaging in this experiment will subconsciously create the changes that they see in their reflection due to the lighting and prolonged period of time that they are staring at themselves. I ask any of you to stare at yourself in a mirror for a few minutes, even in broad daylight, and you'll begin to notice changes in your face, such as the shape or certain features. You may even feel that you don't recognise the person staring back at you if you do it for long enough. Also, when one person starts to describe what they are seeing in the mirror, be that the participant themselves or a guest watching on from behind, it is possible that it then becomes nothing more than the power of suggestion. People will begin to see what they are told is there to see, whether or not that is the case in reality.

It is a fun experiment that can be engaging and interesting for the individuals taking part, but for me, there is very little, if nothing at all, paranormal about most of the "results" gained from conducting a scrying session.

REM Pod

The REM Pod, once explained to our guests, soon becomes one of the favourite pieces of equipment at most investigations, and is certainly one of mine. The device's full name is "Radiating Electromagnetism Pod", so you can see why REM pod is much easier to say. The idea behind this device is that it radiates its own electromagnetic field. This differs from other devices, such as the EMF meter, which detects surrounding electromagnetic fields. Because it radiates its own electromagnetic field, it can detect when something conductive enters in to it, thus changing the strength of the field it is producing. The device uses an antenna for all of this and emits a sound when something is reacting with the electromagnetic field that it is producing. Some people may know of an instrument called a Theremin. If you do then you will know exactly how this device works. Some devices also contain lights which will begin to flash, too, which are similar to an EMF meter in that they are varied in colour, dependant on the strength of the disturbance to the field.

Some models of REM pods can also contain a function called ATDD. This stands for Ambient Temperature Deviation Detection. This function alerts investigators whenever there is a change in temperature, either up or down. If the sound is of a lower pitch, then it is signalling the temperature has dropped and the opposite if the sound is of a higher pitch. A lot of people believe that the occurrence of a cold spot, or warm spot, is linked to the manifestation of a spirit. I have been on investigations where the ATDD has been going mad every couple of seconds as it keeps detecting a rise and fall in the room temperature. Some of these occurrences have happened in locations where the temperature should be stable, with no draughts or windows to cause the sensor to go off.

In an investigation, the REM pod is best used when placed on a table or anywhere out of human interaction. There are times we will carry it around with us, but I am not sure this gives the most accurate results. Some investigators will have several REM pods and, as part of an experiment, will line them up within a room. This is a really good idea to help monitor movement. For example, if a spirit passes one and it triggers the sound and that is followed by the others triggering in turn, then it could be evidence of a spirit moving across the room.

We have experienced, on many occasions, interaction of some kind with our REM pod. Where this piece of equipment can differ to other investigative devices is that it isn't necessarily the centre of attention. Where you will often see investigators sat around an EMF meter or a spirit box, the REM pod is normally left alone. The sound it makes is more than enough to grab our attention and let us know that something is interacting with it, even if we aren't in the vicinity of the device at the time.

One interesting account of using the REM pod happened at a social club we were investigating. A few people had commented on how strange they had felt when stood anywhere on the stairs. Knowing that there had been accounts of activity in this particular area before, we decided to carry out part of our investigation there to see what we could find. In this instance, one of the crew members was holding the REM pod. Once it has calibrated to the person's hand, it doesn't make a sound unless something goes near the device. The team and guests were spread out down the stair case with the REM pod being roughly central on the stairs. People were saying that they could feel a cold air passing them quite frequently, as if someone was walking up and down the staircase. Whenever someone mentioned this, the REM pod would make a sound to let us know something had interfered with its field. This certainly made us feel that there was something moving up and down the staircase, as felt by several of our crew members and guests. During the same investigation, I had constantly been experiencing a really strange feeling that there was someone right behind me, following me everywhere I went within the location. Several times I had turned around expecting to see someone stood there but there had been nothing, or at least there was nobody as close as I had felt there was. Another crew member, unintentionally, had stood near me during the investigation and the REM pod started going off. As I walked away the sound then stopped. A little later, as the crew member approached my back again, it started making a sound. This continued throughout the night, leaving me even more convinced that I was being followed around.

Another great example of the REM pod in action happened at the same time that I had my human pendulum experience at Drakelow Tunnels, which I described earlier. I don't remember much of the experiment, as I have already mentioned, but according to the team and guests that were present, the REM pod was going crazy for the entire duration of the human pendulum experiment and only stopped once I had been helped out of the room. Once I had entered the room again, feeling better than I had felt when leaving, the REM pod started up again, eventually stopping when we all left the room. This certainly left us with the feeling that there was indeed interaction occurring in that specific room.

The thing that I like about the REM pod is that its functionality can't be left entirely down to the human subconscious like experiments such as the human pendulum or spirit walkthrough. Unless the device is broken, or extremely inaccurate, it will only make a sound when something interferes with its electromagnetic field. This is proven by moving your hand closer and further away from the aerial and hearing the sound it makes when your hand is closer. The only time I really find the REM pod can be inaccurate is if it is held by someone when in close proximity to other investigators. Some of the places we visit and investigate have small, tight areas such as cellars, for example. When a group of people are all stood near each other, and I mean almost touching each other at times, there is every chance that the REM pod could be activated simply by someone's elbow brushing past it. This can completely invalidate the effectiveness of such a piece of equipment. Another thing to remember is that, just like the EMF meter, this device can be triggered by things such as mobile phones or walkie talkies. With this in mind, we always ask our group of guests, and crew members for that matter, to ensure their phones are either off or on flight mode. This can help us when trying to validate any evidence that our equipment may give us.

Laser Grid Pen

The laser grid pen, or simply grid pen for short, has recently become a must have piece of equipment for paranormal investigators. It is a very basic piece of equipment when you compare it to the likes of REM pods and EMF meters. The grid pen is used during investigations to help spot any shadows or movement going on in the vicinity that is being investigated.

Essentially, it is a laser pen that comes in different colours; green, red and purple being the most popular. I am sure most people would have had a laser pen as a child. I can remember having one and annoying our neighbours with it by shining it at them when they were out in the garden. Where the grid pen differs to a normal laser pen is that it has a cap on the end that can be adjusted by being turned. This allows the single laser to become a grid of dots. By turning the cap, it will either create a wider grid or bring the dots closer together. This is then aimed at a wall or a doorway, or anywhere where there is suspected movement or shadow activity. The pen itself can either be carried and held by hand or placed on a tripod. The former creates problems, however, because of the risk of movement if held by hand. We find it most useful when it is placed on a tripod when we are investigating wide, open spaced rooms or tunnels. The reason for this is it allows your eyes to see the end of the room, bringing a little more perspective in to the investigation.

We have had successful visual occurrences when carrying out an investigation using a grid pen. More often than not people see shadows passing over the dots within the grid. A lot of investigators, ourselves included, will place a video camera facing the laser grid to record any movement that we may miss with the human eye. For this purpose, the grid pen is beneficial as it can allow for easy detection of movement when watching camera footage back.

This particular piece of equipment requires batteries in order to operate. We had several instances on one investigation where the batteries of our grid pen, along with other equipment such as torches, were drained. The usage of batteries for this one investigation was six AAA batteries. To give that context, our grid pens use two at a time. The one instance saw the grid pen drained of power within five minutes of new batteries being inserted. We even managed to turn this occurrence in to an interesting piece of interaction. At one point, when the strength of the grid pen looked to be diminishing, one crew member asked if a spirit could make the light brighter. Within seconds of the request, the grid pen shone brighter again, as if the batteries were fine. We then asked for the light to be dimmed, and sure enough, it was. This happened several times before the grid pen eventually ran out of battery power. Of course, it is be possible that the grid pen in question here may have been faulty. However, we have never encountered this issue except for this one particular investigation. Also, it is difficult to explain how it was diminishing and brightening upon request, several times. Some theories conclude that spirits use the battery power or electrical power in order to manifest themselves and their energy. Whilst there is no solid proof of this, it is certainly a possible theory when you look at devices such as EMF meters, REM pods and the draining of battery powered equipment.

As with all pieces of investigative equipment, the grid pen is not without its flaws. One issue I find is that if the grid isn't being projected on to a flat surface, the dots can really play with your eyesight. For example, if you are shining the pen at a wall that has an extremely uneven surface or objects in front of it, then the dots will sometimes appear to move by themselves as you move around. This is obviously a form of optical illusion, but is very often treated as paranormal. It also goes without saying that having a laser light projected around a room could mess with an investigator's eyesight, potentially causing them to see shadows or visual disturbances where there are none.

I have heard it argued that there would be more of a chance of seeing shadows and paranormal activity if the lights were switched on during investigations. I have also been asked many times as to why we conduct paranormal investigations in the dead of night with all of the lights switched off. Of course, most people think it is because it is part of the experience and feeling that little bit frightened stood in a creepy place with no light source. I have also heard it explained that it is because spirits tend to be more active at night and between certain hours of the morning. Personally, I have no evidence to substantiate this claim and am a firm believer that spirits can be active and spotted in daylight hours, too. The reason I always give to people who ask why we seem to conduct our experiments on a night time, besides the fact that most investigators have jobs to work during the day, is because when the lights are off and it is pitch black, our other senses really come to the forefront. We rely heavily on our sight when the lights are on and we can easily ignore what our other senses are telling us. However, with the lights off and our ability to see clearly stripped away from us, our other senses become heightened. We begin to feel more, to sense more, to smell more and, most importantly, hear more. Having these senses heightened can be really beneficial when it comes to paranormal investigation. Imagine having sensed something stood next to you during the day, when your vision is at its best, but ignoring it because when you look there is nothing to see. Straight away, the sensation that was felt is brushed aside and forgotten, just because there is nothing to be seen with the eyes. Now imagine the same scenario without any light source and your ability to see taken away. I am sure, in this situation, most people would no longer ignore the sense of something being stood next to them and would begin to use their other heightened senses to "see" what is going on.

Whilst I am a big believer in using your instinct and senses, I can also see a flaw in what I have described above. With the lights off and a potential sense of fear, whether that be fear of the dark, the unknown or a fear of actually having a spirit stood near enough to you that you can sense it, it could be easy to imagine there is something interacting with you. Seeing shadows or sensing interaction could all become tricks of the mind when stood in the dark. Particularly if there is a sense of fear involved.

With all that being said, I think the grid pen can be useful at times, and has proven so with some of our investigations. However, I do not believe it should be used as an integral part of an investigation to gather solid evidence. As with investigational techniques such as calling out, I feel that it leaves too much to the investigator's mind, which could easily begin to play tricks on us if we allow it to, consciously or subconsciously.

EVP Recorder

An EVP recorder is simply a recording device that is used during investigations to try and capture any sounds, such as voices, that the investigators may have missed at the time. EVP stands for Electronic Voice Phenomenon and it is believed that using such a recording device can help capture the words of a spirit, even when the human ear cannot detect anything. To compare the device to something most people will know, I would say it is similar to a dictaphone but with a much better quality of recording.

As with most pieces of equipment, the more you are willing to spend, the better quality the piece of kit will be. For example, EVP recorders can be purchased that include sockets for headphones to be plugged in to as well as a microphone, which will aid the recorder to pick up sounds from further afield. Some will even allow the user to "mark" a point during the live recording to make it easier to find a particular sound you may have heard during the investigation. Believe me when I say that this is a really handy option. It can be really frustrating to have to search through hours of silence or crew chat to find that brief piece of evidence you think you may have caught, only to find it is a guest or crew member coughing.

Along with the EMF meter, an EVP recorder is probably one of the most used pieces of equipment during an investigation and near the top of the list of equipment for any investigator. The initial use for this piece of kit is to capture any sounds or voices that the human ear can't pick up or may have missed. To briefly touch on what I wrote about at the start of the book, if these spirits are operating on a different frequency to us humans, then it is possible that their voices may not be able to be heard by a human ear alone. Take, for example, what I described in the prologue, where we had heard a growl but the EVP recorder had picked up the word hello. With that in mind, the use of this kind of equipment really does aid an investigator in collecting all the possible pieces of evidence available, that they may otherwise have missed.

As with most pieces of equipment, an EVP recorder is best left on a table, chair or any flat, sturdy surface. A lot of investigators will leave several of them around various areas of the location that is being investigated to try and capture anything that could otherwise be missed. They can be held during an investigation, but this can lead to false readings as the recording could pick up sounds such as the investigator breathing or their hand rustling on the recorder itself. If the recorder has been held, then it is important to remember this when listening back to the recordings and analysing potential evidence.

One piece of evidence that we caught on an EVP recorder still amazes me to this day. We were in the cellar of a social club where we were doing some basic calling out and waiting for a response. All of our mobile phones were on flight mode at the time, as well as it being really quite difficult to obtain signal in the cellar area. During the calling out session, someone's phone began to ring. Our first thought was that they had failed to put their phone on to flight mode. However, when we looked at the phone, we could see that it had indeed been on flight mode. A phone should not receive a phone call when in flight mode. Particular in an area where there is very limited phone signal. Also, it was around one in the morning. Combine all of this together and it seems impossible for a phone to be ringing at that moment in time. The calling number was coming up as "Private Number" and the lady refused the call. We continued our investigation and moments later someone else's phone began ringing. This lady wasn't connected to the first person at all. They had met hours before at the beginning of our investigation. The reason I make this point is that my initial reaction was that the person trying to get hold of the first lady had then tried someone else they may have believed would be with the wanted person. Again, the phone was showing "Private Number" and it was on flight mode. She answered the phone and it automatically switched to speaker mode. I have never known a phone do this and, to be honest, I am not sure they can do it automatically. I may be wrong here, but I have never seen it myself. The reason we knew it was on speaker phone was because as soon as she answered, we heard a child's voice. The line was very crackly, sounding similar to static. When the voice spoke, however, it was crystal clear. The voice was definitely that of a young child. Some of us thought it may be a girl, others thought a boy. Personally, I think it sounded like a boy. The accent was a very broad Black Country accent, native to the area we were in. The voice said, "I really want to go home, now." That was it. Once it had said it, the phone went dead. This left the group extremely confused and we kept listening to the EVP over and over again. To this day, I can't seem to come up with an explanation for this occurrence as much as I have tried.

On another investigation, we were using a spirit box and recording the responses on an EVP recorder. We were conducting our investigation around a churchyard and in to the surrounding graveyard. I am not the biggest fan of outdoor investigations. I feel there is far too much chance of noise pollution and false evidence being recorded. When you are in the confines of a building, there is minimum disruption from the outside world, meaning any noise you record or shadows that you see are more than possibly contained within the confines of the building walls. Outside is a different matter. A shadow could be an animal, or another person not partaking in the investigation. A noise could be an animal, the wind and so on. That's not to say, though, that spirits do not appear outside. There are countless sightings reported where a spirit has supposedly been sighted outside, with examples such as battlefields springing to mind, where soldiers are seen seemingly re-enacting their last battle before their death. In this instance, we did capture a solid EVP whilst investigating an outdoor area. We were in the graveyard area and had received a positive response on our spirit box when we asked if there was a Christopher. We had taken the name off a nearby headstone and thought we would ask if he was with us. After several positive responses, we began to ask Christopher if he could move something for us; a stick, for example. After a little bit of static, we heard "I can't" come through on the spirit box. Being keen to gather some physical evidence, we asked him why he couldn't move anything for us. For a while we pressed him for some evidence before we heard "I won't move anything". The voice sounded quite aggravated and we decided to leave that part of the investigation and move on. All three of us had heard that voice and we listened to it several times on the recording, making sure that we were correct in what we thought we had heard. There is always the possibility that we created the words we wanted to hear in our minds and that what we had heard was actually nothing like what I have described. However, for all three of us to confirm we had heard those words and to have them on recording really convinces me that we were right in thinking what we had heard.

I believe the EVP recorder deserves to be a must have in a paranormal investigator's equipment box. There are times that you will think you heard something but wasn't quite sure what it was. This device allows you to go back and listen out for possible evidence. It also allows you to show it to other investigators or friends to see what they think of the evidence. Sometimes this can either help confirm your original thoughts or bring some clarity to the situation and possibly help you see the "evidence" from another perspective. Of course, as with paranormal investigating in general, there is always the possibility that what you have heard or captured could be mixed up within the subconscious to give proof where there isn't any to start with. For example, there are television programmes that show EVP recordings along with subtitles of what is supposedly being said. What I have noticed is that the subtitles confirm to you that the recording is indeed saying what they are telling you it said. I even tried this with my wife when watching one such programme. I covered the subtitles and asked my wife what she thought was being said when the EVP recording was played. She took a guess at what she thought she could hear, but it was no where near what the subtitles read. I then showed her the same recording but with the subtitles. Now that she could read the subtitles and hear the recording at the same time, she changed her mind and stated that the recording did indeed match what the subtitles read. It is this power of suggestion that can easily falsify evidence and make it in to something it never was. If there are a group of people all listening to a recording that they have captured, it is easy for one person's understanding of the recording to soon spread around the group until they all reaffirm what it is that is being said. When conducting an investigation, this sort of behaviour needs to be kept in mind.

Thermal Camera

This piece of equipment is quite rare on the amateur paranormal investigation scene. The reason for this is mainly down to the cost. As with all pieces of equipment, the thermal camera can differ in price, with the higher quality cameras being really quite expensive. It must be said that I really do enjoy using a thermal camera during an investigation. For me, it brings a whole different element to paranormal research. It works by using a camera combined with a thermal lens to detect the infrared light that is around us. Infrared light is part of the light spectrum that is invisible to the human eye. As mentioned at the start of this book, there is a huge amount of the light spectrum that we humans cannot see. When an object is heated up, be that by the sun or a microwave, for example, then the object stores the infrared before slowly distributing it, or cooling down, in some instances. The thermal camera picks up the infrared by displaying warmer objects as a different colour to cooler objects, allowing the investigator to spot anything within the vicinity that is giving off heat. For example, a human being filmed by the camera will be a different colour, or warmer, than the brick wall they may be stood against.

This piece of equipment is best carried around with you whilst conducting the investigation. One thing it can help with is the spotting of "cold spots". People have often used "cold spots" as evidence that a spirit is near. Personally, I can't see how this works. I just don't think enough is known, factually, to see how a ghost appearing or manifesting could translate in to a cold spot being created. However, if a person is adamant that there is a cold spot in a particular area, and I have felt them myself, then the camera should be able to see if what they are feeling is correct. One possible explanation for cold spots is that the person, or persons, experiencing the cold spot could be scared. When in a state of fear, no matter how small, we always seem to have that cold feeling during or after. It could possibly be this that is causing the person to feel a cold spot near them. That being said, if the camera does pick up an area that is showing it to be significantly cooler than the area around it then the person may have found something paranormal. Of course, it could also be a draft, a hole in the wall or another plausible reason. The reason I like this piece of equipment so much, though, is because I can see if the area is cold. If it is, it then allows me to investigate a little further and try and find a reason for it. If I can't find a reason, then there is a chance that it could be paranormal. Maybe.

Just like cold spots, there are also "hot spots" reported. For example, if a person has been sat in a chair for a long time and they get out of the chair, the chair will show as warmer than the surrounding area because of the heat that the person has transferred to the chair. There have been many documented cases, whilst using a thermal camera, where there has been no one sat in a particular chair, and hasn't been all night, but the chair is showing as warm on the camera, as if someone is actually sat, or has recently sat, in the chair. Unless the chair is in front of a radiator or fire, I really struggle to explain how this can happen. I remember speaking to an investigator who said that they could see a chair with a dent in it, as if someone had sat in the chair, squashing the cushion. When they realised no one was there they recorded it with their thermal camera and noticed the whole chair was showing as warm, exactly like it would do if a person was sat in it. To further prove this, they later sat one of their team in the same chair and when they moved out of the chair it was showing as warm, just like before.

It is this kind of evidence that makes me really enjoy working with the thermal camera. Investigators just need to be careful and make sure that they have eliminated any possible causes for hot or cold spots, such as drafts, before jumping to conclusions that it is paranormal.

IR Thermometer

This piece of equipment is a cheaper version of the thermal camera and features more on the amateur investigation scene. Just like the camera, it reads temperatures that are being given off by infrared. The difference between the two pieces of equipment, and the main reason in cost difference, is that this one doesn't have a camera. It takes readings by the user holding a trigger and pointing the emitting laser at a specific area in order to gain a temperature reading which is displayed on a small screen on the thermometer.

It goes without saying that the thermal camera is much better to use for investigators looking to find visual evidence. However, the IR thermometer is just as good at reading temperatures, so can come in handy when a hot or cold spot is being felt, or someone says that their hand is cold, for example.

We have used this piece of kit quite often and it has helped us several times to prove that someone is actually experiencing a rush of coldness or heat. It must be said that the heat experience is very rare when compared to cold spots. We often have guests say that their hand feels cold, as if someone has touched it. By pointing the laser at the person, we can ascertain if that particular part of their body differs at all when compared to others in the area.

Whilst both of these items of equipment can be great fun to use and can give up some good evidence, try to remember what I mentioned earlier in this section. There is, in my opinion, no evidence that directly relates spirits to the sudden appearance of hot or cold spots. With this in mind, I would always recommend trying to find a plausible reason for why there is a hot or cold spot before considering it to be anything remotely paranormal.

Dowsing Rods

Dowsing rods, otherwise known as divining rods, have been used for centuries as a means of finding a source of water, any buried items such as metals and most recently within the paranormal world as a way of contacting spirits. The material of the rods themselves vary. People have used many different materials including branches off trees, the wire from a coat hanger or lengths of copper. The traditional shape of the rod was a Y shape, with the two ends being held one in each hand, pointing the bottom of the Y away from the body. The idea was that the Y would begin to shake or dip whenever the person holding it was near to a water source. As time has gone on, people have begun to use more of an L shaped rod. For this, the user holds the shorter end of the L and points the long end away from their body just like a gun would be held, again one in each hand. The idea is to not hold the rods too tightly, or else you may prevent them from moving in your hands at all. There are differing views and opinions on what should happen to the L shaped rods once a water source, or in our case, a spirit is found. For some people, they believe that the rods cross over each other. For others, only one rod may cross over. Some people believe that the best material to use when dowsing is copper. The reason for this is that the material is very conductive, second only to silver, which is a lot more expensive than copper. A common misconception is that gold has a higher conductivity rate than copper, but this isn't true. The idea behind using a conductive material is that the energy surrounding us will be absorbed in to the rods, allowing the spirits to use the energy and manipulate the movements of the rods in order to answer our questions. It is a common belief amongst paranormal investigators and believers in general that spirits require energy in order to manifest themselves. This could be why batteries are drained or electrical equipment appears faulty whenever paranormal activity seems to be occurring.

When conducting this experiment, we always tell the participants to obtain a yes and no answer in their minds. You can speak out loud, but when there are a number of people taking part in the experiment, it can become a bit noisy and messy. I have even heard it claimed that someone's dowsing rods were answering someone else's questions that were being asked aloud. The answers can be different from person to person, just like with the human pendulum, where some people sway forward for a yes and others may sway backwards. Once the answers have been obtained, we then ask the participants to begin their questioning and monitor the answers that they are receiving. It is very rare that the people taking part in the dowsing do not get an answer to their questions in one way or another. For some people, their rods will cross for a yes and swing apart for a no, or vice versa.

I have taken part in this experiment numerous times and have had the rods seemingly answering my questions. Interestingly, I always seem to get the same yes answer and no answer when first starting the experiment. Is it possible that my subconscious is answering the questions I am asking and that there is no spirit at all interacting with the rods that I am holding? I would say it is absolutely possible.

It came as no surprise to me to learn that this kind of experiment is seen as a pseudoscience and has no basis in any scientific research. I would say that this experiment could be heavily influenced by the ideomotor effect. As mentioned previously, this is where a person makes subconscious, or even unconscious, movements or motions. In this instance, the participant may be absolutely adamant that they are not personally responsible for the movement of the dowsing rods in their hands, but it could be that they are subject to the ideomotor effect and are fully responsible for the movement, they just don't know it.

Because of this, I really find it hard to believe that any response from a moving dowsing rod is the reaction to a question being answered by a spirit. I believe that the participant is fully responsible, whether aware of it or not, for the movement of the rods.

Pendulums

I have included pendulums within the dowsing rods section as they are a similarly conducted experiment. Pendulums are usually made of crystals, but can be made of wood or metal, and are attached to a chain, sometimes silver in material, allowing the pendulum to swing freely when held. People who use pendulums often say that they will use pendulums that they were drawn to. The idea being that the particular crystal that their pendulum contains has a certain quality that they are drawn to and therefore offers the best results when used. I have even heard people claim that they won't get responses from spirits if they are not using their own pendulum. Pendulums, with their varying crystals, are often used as a form of dowsing during healing sessions such as Reiki, where they are used to seek out any bad energy contained within an individual and help remove it so that it can be replaced with a higher vibrational energy.

When used during a paranormal investigation to try and contact spirits, the pendulum is held freely from the hand and questions are asked, just like with the dowsing rods. Again, different people will have different responses to their yes and no answer. Just like with the dowsing rods, I always seem to have the same response for a yes and for a no. A circular swinging motion will normally represent a no for me, whilst a yes response is usually signified by the pendulum swinging in a straight line.

My thoughts on this experiment are exactly the same as the dowsing rods, so I won't repeat myself. However, I have recently started venturing in to the world of crystals and have started to use them during my meditation sessions. I have yet to see any firm results from using crystals against not using them whilst mediating, but I do have an interesting theory as to why people may feel certain vibrational effects from crystals. If the world is made up of objects that are all vibrating to a certain frequency in order to exist, then the crystals must also be vibrating to a particular frequency. Could it be that the frequency the crystals are vibrating at have a resonance with the vibrational frequency of the people who are drawn to particular crystals and are affected by them, in a positive or negative way? It is certainly worth thinking about and looking further in to, in my opinion.

Table Tipping

Table tipping, also referred to as table tilting or table turning, originally came to the forefront during the 1800's. During this time, it was common for people to conduct seances, where a group of people would sit around a table with their hands placed palms down upon the surface of the table. Once in position, the group would ask questions aloud and await a response. There were times, supposedly, where the spirits would respond by rotating or moving the table.

Table tipping in modern paranormal investigations is similar in how it is conducted. Several people will stand or sit around a small table and place their hands lightly on top of the table. Some people prefer to press lightly with their fingertips, not wanting to put the whole of their hand upon the table. Personally, I prefer this way as it means there is less physical contact between the person and the table, meaning it is more difficult to fake the experiment.

I have participated in this experiment several times and watched it from a distance. There have been times the table has moved quite violently, causing the participants to move around the room just to keep in contact with the table. What fascinates me the most about this experiment is how I have seen the table move with my own eyes but could not see any outside influence from any of the participants who, as I initially thought, may have been moving the table themselves.

I have heard this experiment be put in to the ideomotor effect category with the likes of the human pendulum or automatic handwriting. Whilst I can see the validity of the latter two experiments being put down to the ideomotor effect and the subconscious movements of an individual, I can't bring myself to see how this could relate to table tipping, just as I struggle to explain the results of a spirit board. I can completely understand, and get on board, with how the ideomotor effect can be used to explain away the results of the human pendulum. For example, if one person wishes to answer yes or no, whether consciously or not, they can and that is the result you will get from the experiment. However, with table tipping, just as with the spirit board, there is a vastly low chance that all of the people participating in the experiment will want to spell out the same name or move the table in a particular way or direction. If all of the people involved with the table tipping experiment have nothing more than their fingers lightly pressed upon the surface of the table, with nothing whatsoever beneath the table, then I really struggle to explain how the table could move in any way at all, let alone be lifted several inches from the floor or dragged around the room, as I have personally witnessed. If this isn't an interaction from a spirit then we must surely be talking about some form of telekinesis which is equally as dumbfounding as the possibility that a spirit from an invisible realm is responsible for moving the table or spelling out names and answers on a spirit board.

Just like the spirit board, this experiment, when conducted correctly and is giving results, is an absolute wonder to witness and be a part of.

The Pub

I spent a few of my teenage years living in a pub that my mum and dad ran. Unfortunately, the pub is no longer there, making way for two houses. Nearly all pubs come with stories of hauntings and strange things happening, and this was no exception.

The lay out of the pub was ordinary. A bar, a lounge, a cellar and an upstairs area where we lived. The bar was tiled and had the usual dart board, pool table and jackpot machine. The lounge had a carpet and the seats were better upholstered. We also had the basement where the beer cellar was. It was adjacent to a small room where I used to keep my drum kit. Before the pub opened on weekends I'd go down and practise the drums. I would stick my headphones in and drum along to my favourite songs. The room I was in had a door at the top of a ramp and this is where the barrels of beer would be rolled down in to the cellar before being moved in to the section where the barrels were connected to the pipes. It was here that I had two strange events occur.

On one Saturday morning, whilst playing the drums, there were some barrels stood against the wall opposite, stacked on top on one another, two high. Whilst drumming away I happened to look up at the barrels, only to see them shifting from left to right. There were six barrels and all of them were moving together. I stopped playing straight away, as I couldn't believe what I was seeing, and the barrels stopped moving. I then began to drum again and the barrels began to move again. At first, I found this strange but then quickly put the occurrence down to the fact that the only way they could move was down to the vibration of the drums causing the empty barrels to move across the floor. With this in mind, I decided to carrying on playing the drums and try to forget about what had happened. Sure enough, as soon as I started my drumming again, the barrels moved along to the beat. My drumming sessions usually last around an hour before I got bored and headed back upstairs. On this occasion, before I headed back upstairs, I decided to check if the barrels were indeed empty. To my amazement, they were full! These were full barrels of beer. Full barrels of beer that were moving along to my drumming. Any of you who have ever tried to move a full barrel of beer will understand why I was so shocked that these had all been moving in time to my drumming. If they were empty then I could kind of understand how that would be possible due to the vibration of my drum kit but the fact that they were full really left me confused. There were many more occasions following this that I went down to play the drums, but never again did this happen.

I often used to work behind the bar to help out my parents, which I didn't mind as I would get paid and it meant I could socialise with the locals, who on the whole were nice people and there were times that it was just me behind the bar if my parents had gone out or were upstairs. Although the pub was split in to two rooms, the bar that serviced both rooms ran along both. There were several times that

I was in the bar, either watching TV or talking to a customer, when a beer mat would be thrown from the lounge, along the bar and land at my feet. The first couple of times this happened I made my way in to the lounge thinking that it could be a customer wanting my attention, but when I got to the lounge there was never anyone there. The next couple of times it happened I decided to race out of the bar hoping to catch a kid who was possibly playing but there was never anyone in sight. This happened frequently but I never felt threatened or scared by the activity. It seemed to be very playful and light hearted. My brother, who is four years younger than me, didn't quite feel the same about the place. He would very often share my bed, claiming that his room "had a man in". I would leave him in my room from time to time and sleep in his, yet I never felt the presence of a man, or anything else that may have contributed to his fear of sleeping in there.

The best activity that occurred during our time living in the pub happened, as most instances of paranormal activity do, in the middle of the night. It was one of the nights that I had left my brother in my room and went to sleep in his bed. My dad woke me up in the early hours, saying my mum thought someone had broken in to the pub and wanted us to check it out. Apparently, she could hear noises coming from down in the bar area. The location of the pub was quite well known for thefts, our own car having been stolen several months previous to this night. We made our way down the corridor and to the top of the stairs, stopping to pick up my brother's cricket bat along the way. Once we had opened the door at the top of the stairs, we could make out noises coming from the bar area. We carefully, and almost reluctantly, descended the stairs which led to a door that took you behind the bar. At this point we could hear a lot of noise. Glasses were sliding across the bar, stools were being banged and dragged across the tiled floor and what sounded like pool balls hitting each other. Interestingly, there were no voices to be heard at all.

The light behind the bar could be switched on and off by a switch the other side of the door and I remember telling my dad to flick the switch at the same time I burst through the door. The reason being, that if a light came on first, they could be out of the pub before we were through the door and in to the bar. We timed it to perfection. I burst through the door as the light came on. What I found, however, was a perfectly tidy, silent pub. All of the glasses were in their place beneath the bar. The stools were upside down and placed on top of the table, as they were each and every night. The pool table was empty. The front door was locked with no sign of anyone being in the pub. We even checked the toilets and the cellar but found nothing. Eventually we decided to head back to bed. Not that I did much sleeping! Again, just like with the drum instance, this never happened again.

It was a sad day when we left and I wish I knew then what I know now about the investigative techniques and associated equipment. An investigation conducted properly in this pub, I believe, would have definitely given some great results. Unfortunately, as the pub is no longer standing, I can't even look at returning. Maybe the houses that now stand in its place are experiencing some strange occurrences.

The Ship

My dad served several years in the Royal Navy and was unfortunate enough to have to participate in the Falklands war. His main job on the ship was as an engineer, his correct title being Marine Engineering Mechanic. The slang word for this was a Stoker. One of his duties included having to take lubrication oil readings each shift. From what he has told me, this would happen through the night, too, so some engineers would be resting or sleeping whilst others worked the night shift.

In order to record the lubrication oil readings, he had to descend the ladders in to the plummer block compartment of the ship. The plummer block is a rather integral part of a ship as it is where the engine's drive shaft goes through the hull of the ship. The propeller is then attached on the external side of the ship, or hull. This task was carried out a lot, so my dad would have done this many times himself already.

One night, whilst taking the readings in the plummer block, a voice called down to him from the top of the ladders asking if everything was ok. He looked up the ladders to see a man stood there in full uniform looking down at him. My dad, being relatively new to this ship, assumed this man was the Chief Stoker. Upon seeing him at the top of the ladders, towards the compartment hatch, my dad responded that everything was fine and that there were no problems to report. At this, he went back to taking the oil sample and readings. Interestingly, he never heard the Chief Stoker leave. No footsteps or anything that would indicate he left the vicinity.

Once he had finished his task, he returned to the Machine Control Room and asked one of his colleagues who the Chief Stoker was that night. His colleague responded with a smile and said, "oh, you've met him then?". My dad asked what his name was as he hadn't seen him on the ship before and his colleague went on to explain that my dad had met the resident ghost. Naturally, my dad took this as a joke, but it was backed up by other colleagues. My dad also never saw that particular Chief Stoker again.

Having spoken to my dad at great length about this, he explained how the man had appeared as a solid person who looked like any living man would have looked stood at the top of the ladder. I asked him if it was possible that one of the lads had played a trick on him and pretended to be this man. He said that it *was* possible but he would have known by looking at the man. The other thing worth considering is that if this Chicf Stokcr was indeed a living, breathing man serving on the ship at the same time as my dad, why didn't they cross paths again? It isn't like the Chief Stoker could have got very far as, seeing how they were out at sea at the time, they were all restricted to the confines of the ship. Either way, this certainly spooked my dad who, despite looking for this man, never saw him again.

The Local

Since my wife and I have moved in to our new home, I have been frequenting the local pub. As I became more of a regular face in there, I began to strike up conversations with the bar staff and the landlord, some about the history of the building. As a paranormal investigator, I managed to steer the conversation towards whether or not the building was haunted and, if so, had any of the staff or customer ever experienced something paranormal. Straight away, the landlord got very excited to be having a conversation on this topic, and rushed straight in to telling me all about the activity that he, and the staff, had experienced. Some of the staff claimed to have seen a shadow passing through the kitchen wall in to the bar area. There have been claims of more shadow like figures coming out of the men's toilet area and through the bar. This particular claim has also affected me. Whilst sitting in the corner of the room, with the toilet door to my right, there have been numerous occasions I have caught the glimpse of what I thought was someone emerging from the toilet yet no one walks past me and out of the room. This was one of the reasons I wanted to investigate this location. There have also been witnesses of boxes flying off the shelf, things being thrown behind the bar from a seemingly empty room and names of bar staff being called out when they are alone. Interestingly, my wife, who is a stone-cold sceptic of anything paranormal, has even experienced something here. We were out to watch a local band playing and were stood at the back of the room. No one could walk behind us because of how close to the wall we were. Whilst watching the band, she felt something brush her lower back as if someone had either run their hand across it or someone had brushed past her. Obviously, nothing was there and she was left a little confused as to what it could have been. She is still a sceptic, but I must admit that I did enjoy seeing her face after this had happened and hearing her try to explain what it possibly could have been. Furthermore, the area of the wall we were stood in front of is the exact same area of the wall that staff have seen a shadow pass through.

After many conversations about setting up an investigation, we finally agreed on a time and date. From a personal point of view, there was a lot of trepidation about investigating a pub. One of my main concerns was that of the guests being intoxicated before the investigation started and the potential of this ruining the night for the staff, crew members and anyone who genuinely wanted to conduct a serious investigation. The landlord and I agreed that should there be anyone who appears to be intoxicated and wanting to make fun of the investigation, then we would evict them from the location.

This is something really worth considering when conducting paranormal investigations. What we eat and drink may have an effect on how we perceive the investigation. For example, if you were to drink an energy drink beforehand, or during an investigation, it will most certainly affect your body in terms of heart rate and may give headaches amongst other immediate effects to the consumer. Some people may mistake these symptoms as paranormal. Likewise, if sugary food is consumed around the time of an investigation, it may affect the body and how the consumer perceives a situation that may occur throughout the night. There's certainly something to be said for conducting some more research in to this particular area of paranormal investigating.

All of that being said, the guests on the night were fantastic and very respectful to the crew, the landlord and staff as well as the whole occasion itself.

The crew decided to use minimal equipment during this investigation, partly due to not knowing what kind of reception we would receive from the guests, as spoken about above, but also because the location isn't the biggest and we wanted to really bring it back to basics where equipment is concerned. We ended up using a spirit board in two specific locations, a spirit box, an infrared motion sensor alongside a camera in the kitchen area where the shadow had been seen walking through the wall, a hand held camera and we conducted a human pendulum in both bar areas.

The camera and infrared motion sensor didn't capture anything throughout the night, which was disappointing. The spirit board, however, proved to be extremely active in both of the areas that it was conducted. What was really interesting was that the two groups who participated in the board at different intervals throughout the night both yielded similar results, with the same name being given to both groups. The name belonged to a customer of the pub who had sadly died two weeks previous to the investigation, but it seems he may still be visiting the pub in the afterlife. Another visit on the board seemed to come from one of the guest's late husband, who had passed on around eight years before. According to the lady, she had been to see several mediums previously and Bob had always come through as quite an impatient spirit who wanted to be heard. This seemed to be the case again here. After several minutes of speaking with Bob on the spirit board, the group asked him to move on and allow other spirits the chance to communicate. Bob didn't like this, it seems, and continued to occupy the spotlight until the lady suggested she remove herself form the room to give other spirits a chance. Once she did leave the room, so did Bob, and the group began communicating with the customer mentioned above. The spirit board also seemed to bring through one of the guest's grandad and another guests nan. Both seemed shocked to have had a "visit" by one of their relatives, with one answering some very distinct questions correctly. I think it is important to point out that although both groups got the same name, that of the customer, neither groups had conversed about what they had experienced until the end of the investigation.

The human pendulum yielded some interesting results, also, despite my reservations on the experiment. Besides the instance I mentioned in the human pendulum chapter where a lady who wasn't initially participating in the experiment became the centre of attention, this also gave Bob another chance to shine. This time it was the landlord participating who seemed to be under the influence of Bob. After several minutes of asking Bob to allow others to come forward, and a stern word from his wife, he finally seemed to leave the vicinity and allow a female spirit to come through. The female spirit, once questioned, revealed that she had lived in the pub when it was a cottage a few centuries ago, and that she had died in her seventies. We also managed to find out that she was a farmer on the land, which specialised in sheep, which, through post investigation research, has been proven true.

For me, on a personal level, the most intriguing area that we investigated was the cellar. When we first descended down the steps in to the cellar, the noise of the air conditioning and ice machine motor was verging on deafening. I initially thought that the area would prove to be quiet, particularly for audible evidence, as the loud noise would prevent anyone from hearing anything, and may even distract us from any other activity that may occur whilst down there. It didn't take long before I was proven very wrong. The area itself was a strange layout. The area at the bottom of the steps, small square area, was used to store empty barrels waiting for collection and full barrels waiting to be used. At the other end of the cellar was a similar sized and shaped area where the barrels were in use, the pipes leading from the barrels and running up through the ceiling in to the bar area. Connecting the spaces was a thin corridor around fifteen metres long, just wide enough to walk down without touching the walls either side. It was also a low ceiling, with no room to stand upright anywhere for anyone of average height. We decided to place some bar stools down the corridor, with a few in both areas either side. Once settled down, the noise that had worried me initially seemed to fade in to the background as our ears became accustomed to it. The first bit of activity we encountered whilst down there was what sounded like a banging. This happened a few times before stopping. This was then replaced by a whistle. A very audible whistle that responded to me when prompted. I asked for the whistle to be repeated at least four times and each time I was answered with a very loud, brief whistle. The activity then moved to the bottom area where barrels sounded like they were moving. Interestingly, these barrels were the ones in use, so wouldn't be light. At the time of them moving, we had placed a guest in the corner as there had been previous reports of activity in that particular area. The barrel that was moving was right in front of her. This happened around five times before I decided to get a picture of the area. I could not have timed the photo better, because as soon as my flash lit up the cellar, everyone in the area saw the barrel rock from side to side, proving that it was the barrel making the noise we had been hearing. When leaving the cellar, I checked the area for any uneven flooring, which there wasn't, or to see if the barrel was easily moved, which it wasn't. Very strange indeed.

Although, the strangest occurrence in the cellar was when my name was called, loud enough to be heard over the air conditioning units and running motors. As I was moving down the corridor checking that everyone was ok, I distinctly heard "Kieran, come here" from behind me. I instinctively turned around and asked if everyone was ok, thinking one of the guests had called me. None of them had, but several of them had also heard the voice that I had heard. The tone of the voice wasn't aggressive, but more authoritative, as if a parent was telling their misbehaving child to "come here". This particular occurrence is one of the best audible experiences I have encountered on a paranormal investigation to date. As with most pieces of paranormal activity, it is always a great feeling to not only experience something, but to have other people also experience it and be able to validate your claims and prove you were not wrong in hearing, seeing, or feeling what you do.

This location really did throw some interesting activity at us throughout the course of the night and we have made sure to arrange future events, as I believe it will only become more active with each investigation carried out there.

The House

When I was around the age of eight, my family moved homes. We left behind the home I mentioned earlier where my mum's nan would frequently visit us and moved in to a new house not far away. Although not paranormal in nature, a strange story does surround the move. Once my parents had finalised the paperwork to move, my dad told my grandad that we had moved to this particular street. Upon hearing the name of the street, my grandad pointed out that he and his siblings were born on that street. As if this wasn't a strange enough coincidence, he then revealed that the house we were moving in to was indeed the very house that he had been born in and had spent a portion of his childhood in. What a very strange occurrence. If you believe in fate, or as I call it, synchronicity, then you may say it was meant to be.

Shortly after moving in to the new house, my dad's aunt passed away. I don't have many memories of her but one memory I do have is of her unique smell. Having been a school dinner lady for most of her life, she seemed to emanate an odour that was a mixture of grease and perfume. It wasn't long after she had passed away that our family had begun to smell this odour at certain points throughout the day, with the most common time being first thing in the morning. I remember my mum would wake up, walk down stairs and I would hear her saying "morning, Beryl". Another thing we noticed was that my mum's nan hadn't appeared to follow us from our old home to our new one and my parents believed it was because she didn't wish to be treading on the toes of my dad's family, with the new house being where his family had been born and raised. This would also explain why Beryl had returned to this house.

Since moving in, apart from the strange, yet familiar, smell we get every now and then, there has been numerous occurrences that seem to fall within the realms of paranormal activity. One such piece of activity involved some of Beryl's ornaments that she had left behind. One morning my mum woke on the sofa, where she goes to read if she is having trouble sleeping and could hear a rattling sound. At first, she thought it was simply the gerbil moving around his cage and exercising on his wheel. After a few more seconds of hearing this noise she ruled out the gerbil as it sounded much closer. She cast her eyes across the living room, trying to find the source of the noise, before finally seeing that it was a pair of candle holders that were moving across the table. She sat and stared for around thirty seconds whilst the candle holders shook their way from one end of the table to the next.

Another incident that involved my mum happened when she was ironing in the kitchen. She had a strange sensation that someone was watching her, which I am sure most of us have experienced at one time or another. When she looked up from the ironing board and out of the kitchen window, which faced our back garden, she could see the back of a man standing outside the window staring down the garden. She described him as wearing a flat cap but couldn't see anything below his shoulders due to the window. She went outside to ask him who he was but he had vanished by the time she got there. Around three months after this, she was pottering around in the garden and again had this feeling that someone was staring at her. She turned around to see what looked like the same man, who again had his back to her, and was this time staring up our driveway towards the front of the house. This time she could see his body and described him as wearing clothes that would be typical of the early 1900's, including his flat cap. She stared at him for a few seconds and carried on with her gardening. When she glanced back shortly after, he was gone. None of our family have any idea who this man is or why he keeps appearing in our garden. Also, why is it only my mum who can see him and why does he have his back to her every time he appears?

Until recently we had a family dog, who unfortunately passed away around a year before the release of this book. She was a lovely dog, who loved a fuss from anyone willing to give her attention and would spend most of her time lying at the feet of my dad in the living room. Her bed was in the kitchen area and she would often go there if it was really late at night and someone was still up watching the TV. I guess it was her way of getting some peace and quiet. One night, whilst I watching a late-night film, she came darting out of the kitchen and sat in the doorway, staring towards her bed, growling. I tried to get her attention but she was so focused on whatever was going on in the kitchen that she didn't respond to me. After a brief moment, she tilted her head and then seemed to follow something from left to right. From where I was sat, I could see in to the kitchen, yet could see nothing that would make her act like she was. It was as if something had startled her and she could see whatever it was moving around the kitchen. Eventually, she calmed down and after a fuss, returned to her bed. There seems to be a lot of incidents where people's pets seem to be watching something that can't be seen by their human owners. Is it possible that they can access frequencies or parts of the light spectrum that we cannot? For example, a recent study has stated that it is possible that dogs can see in ultraviolet. It has already been agreed that birds and reptiles can see in ultraviolet, a section of the light spectrum that the human eye requires equipment for in order to see. With that in mind, it is very possible that our dog was watching a spirit moving around the kitchen even though I could see nothing.

Another late night threw up a very strange incident for my brother and my dad. Both were sat watching TV, with the dog lying at my dad's feet. Suddenly, a bright light caught their eye as it moved through the living room curtains. I have asked them both to describe the light, imagining it to be similar to a spotlight on a wall created by a torch. Both have stated that it wasn't like that, but more like a solid ball of light, similar to an orb and around the size of a football. It came through the curtains at around five feet off the ground, before quickly dropping down to just a few inches off the floor. It then made its way through the living room and in to the kitchen. Both sat and stared in amazement at this ball of light, whilst the dog got up and followed it as it made its way in to the kitchen. However, the dog stopped at the doorway and didn't seem to want to go any further. Instead, she stared in to the kitchen for a short while before resuming her spot near my dad. I have asked my brother what he thought this was but he doesn't seem to have an answer. It most certainly does come across as a very strange occurrence, and one that I wish I had been able to witness myself.

This wasn't the first and only time that this ball of light has appeared. Around a year later, my parents were sat out in the garden enjoying their morning coffee. At this point the family dog had passed away. If she was still alive, she would have no doubt been wondering around the lawn and barking at birds as they landed on the fence. Whilst staring down towards the bottom of the garden, my mum noticed a ball of light, similar to the one witnessed by my brother and my dad, moving slowly up the garden towards where they were sat. she described it as being around a foot off the grass and moving slowly and deliberately. She managed to get my dad's attention and they both sat watching this light move towards them. It eventually reached the patio area, where it travelled between the flowerpots and around the back of their chairs before vanishing. Both of them believe that this was a manifestation of the dog. The reason for this is the light seemed to take the exact route that the dog would take when moving up the garden. It was a route she would take so frequently that there was actually a line in the grass where she would walk. Despite being told not to, she would also always push her way through the flowerpots, knocking a few flowers off in the process, before moving over to whoever was sat outside at the time for a bit of a fuss. The movement of the orb certainly does match that of the dog and it would be nice to think that it was her just enjoying the early morning sunshine and taking her usual route up the garden. However, if the light is the same as the one witnessed in the living room, and we can't be certain it is, but if so, then it can't be the dog because she was still alive when the first incident occurred. The first thing that I thought it could have been on both occasions is ball lightning. However, there was no sign of a thunderstorm on either occasion, and witnesses of ball lightning often describe it exploding and leaving behind a smell of sulphur. Neither of these happened. Although my parents believe the second incident was the family dog, we can't be completely sure, but I am sure we can agree that both incidents were very strange indeed.

Most of the activity seems to happen downstairs, particularly in the kitchen area. Whether it is because I know this or because I am picking up on the energy, I have always had the feeling that I have not been alone when in the kitchen. The upstairs of the house has always felt fine and devoid of such energy, but I was always hesitant if I needed a late-night drink and had to venture to the kitchen.

I have now moved out of the house and have been living with my wife for some years, but I will conduct an investigation of sorts at some point in the near future, to see if I can dig a little deeper in to what exactly is causing the strange phenomena we have all experienced there.

The Cottage

One of my close friends recently moved in to a quaint little cottage in one of the nearby towns. It is a strange location as you enter the street because it is directly off a busy road, really close to a large supermarket and busy high street. However, as soon as you enter the street, it really is like being transported back a couple of hundred years. It seems to be the remains of a hamlet, a smaller version of a village, with a couple of the homes having been renovated and modernised over time. Although the cottage has had a lot of work done to it, mainly for the health and safety of the people residing in it, it does appear to have kept its charm, as well as a few other ghostly things of the past, it seems.

The cottage itself was used as a prison back in the day and, even now, still has the original cell and bars in place, which makes for a great talking point for any visitors. My friend soon learned that his work manager had also grown up on the same street, with his parents still living in the house a few doors away. Once my friend pointed out the strange incidents that he and his partner had encountered, his manager couldn't stop talking about all of the sightings and experiences that he and his family had come across over the years. It is apparently common knowledge to all of the residents that there is a policeman who still patrols the little street from time to time, having even been spotted with his oil lamp as he makes his way around the houses. It would make sense that this policeman was based in the station that is now the cottage where my friend resides.

One of the first experiences occurred not long after they had moved in. He was stood at the kitchen sink, washing up, when a shadow caught his attention outside. He looked up from the crockery and out of the window to see a black shadow walk across the window, from left to right. I asked my friend if he noticed any distinct features on the shadow or any features at all, for that matter. He said that the shadow had a three-dimensional feel to it, as if it was a solid object, and had the shape of a human, but was just a black mass. He watched it for the few seconds it took for the shadow to get passed the window before leaning out of the window to try and follow it, but to no avail. The very first thing he thought it could be was someone looking to break in, which, of course, had him worried. However, no one did break in and he was left feeling a little confused as to what he had seen. When he next saw his manager, he pointed this encounter out to him and asked for his opinion. The opinion was that it could have been the policeman doing his nightly rounds. This seems to be the explanation that my friend has since stuck to, believing it to be the policeman showing the new residents that he is there to look after them and they don't have to worry.

Not long after this sighting, my friend had returned home from work to find that his kitchen chairs had been pulled in to the middle of the room, and one of his bags, which is usually placed upon one of the chairs, was on the floor on the other side of the room. Of course, he asked his partner if she had been responsible for this but she denied it, which was easy enough to believe, as she had been at work all day and had yet to return home. Couple this incident with the many doors they have heard banging throughout the night from time to time and it is easy to see why they believe the house has a ghostly resident.

However, just as the residents of this street all believe, it definitely seems to be the outside of the house that has more incidents. One resident even quoted as saying "it's not what is on the inside that matters, but the outside". This may seem a little dramatic, but you get what he is trying to say. My friend's partner had the second visible experience, similar to the first. She had moved over to the bedroom window in order to draw the curtains and prepare for bed. When she reached the window and looked down in to the street outside the house, she saw a man stood beneath the streetlight staring at the house, wearing a long overcoat. Again, there were no distinct features to the man. She described the figure as looking like a man with the way it was stood and the build and stature. Of course, this frightened her and she told my friend straight away, who looked out the window himself shortly after but there was no-one stood where she had seen the figure previously. Again, my friend reported this to his manager. When he was explaining the incident to him, his manager interrupted him and made a bet that he could finish the story word for word. This left my friend speechless as he listened to his manager explain where this figure was stood, how he looked, what he was wearing and what he was doing. It turns out that most of the residents, my friend's manager included, have had this sighting, and they have all put it down to it being the police officer keeping a watchful eye on his area. Of course, it could very well be a man who is scoping out the street for future burglaries, but these sightings have been occurring over the course of three to four decades, all of the same man, in the same clothes, in the same spot. A very strange street indeed, and one that I'm looking to investigate in the near future, if the residents will allow me.

Epilogue

The idea behind this book was to put across what happens on paranormal investigations and what to expect should you ever attend one yourself. I also wanted to put across some of the current techniques that we use and equipment that is used on investigations, so that anyone who wishes to start out investigating themselves should have a better understanding of what is out there to use and how to use it in order to attempt to contact any spirits. I hope this has come across throughout the book and that you now have a better understanding of paranormal investigating, the equipment and the techniques, should you be looking at starting out in the field for the first time. If you are a seasoned investigator, or someone with more experience, then maybe this book has shown you new ways of thinking. Either way, I hope that it has been an enjoyable read.

With that being said, I would like to say that to anyone who regularly attends or conducts paranormal investigations, all of the above contains my own thoughts and opinions, and I respect those of other people, even if they differ from mine. One of the reasons I became involved in this field was to meet new people who shared my interests and curiosity, who I could have discussions with and learn from. I hugely believe that we should always keep an open mind and be open to taking on board new ideas, new theories and new techniques, particularly if it helps advance the field of paranormal investigating.

Far too often people claim to have the definitive answer on what exactly is going on when it comes to the paranormal, but can we ever truly be sure? We can theorise and we can debate, using evidence collected when out investigating, but I am not convinced that anyone yet has the answer to questions such as; What are spirits? How do they manifest? Are they actually deceased people, or potentially entities that never even lived in our world? These are the questions, along with many more, that we should be working towards answering when conducting paranormal investigations. However, for these sorts of questions to be answered, I believe we need to move on from old techniques, some of which I have mentioned in this book, and look towards using new technology, new techniques and adopt a fresh way of thinking. Only by doing this will we ever move forward and begin to understand, at least a little better, what exactly it is that we are dealing with when we are in contact with a spirit.

This is where the next part of my research and investigating is going to be taking me, where I will be looking at new ways of investigating and communicating with spirits and will be attempting to bring in some fresh ideas and techniques in order to advance our investigations and, hopefully, collect more evidence that shows spirits do actually exist, as well as trying to have a better understanding of what exactly it is we are communicating with when we believe we are dealing with a spirit.

To those readers who regularly conduct paranormal investigations and regularly research the field, I hope you continue to do so with an open mind and a thirst for fresh ideas, new theories and a constant need for evidence, and of course, most of all, continue to enjoy what you do and have fun! For those readers who are just looking at beginning their journey in to the world of paranormal investigating, I hope you stay safe and enjoy the ride. There are certainly going to be some very interesting, possibly scary, but definitely thought-provoking occurrences right around the corner, and I am sure you will enjoy every minute of it, as I know I do!

<u>THE END</u>

About Kieran Woodhouse

Kieran is an England based paranormal investigator, a public speaker on the subject and a co-host of the Paranormal Paradigm Podcast. Kieran can be reached via his email address kieran.woodhouse@gmail.com or via the podcast email address: paranormalparadigmpodcast@gmail.com. Please feel free to contact him regarding any stories or information about the world of the paranormal or regarding any investigations.

Printed in Great Britain
by Amazon